THE DEVOLUTION OF JIHADISM

From Al Qaeda to Wider Movement

STRATFOR
221 W. 6th Street, Suite 400
Austin, TX 78701

Printed in the United States of America

The contents of this book originally appeared as analyses
on STRATFOR's subscription Web site.

ISBN: 1453746641
EAN-13: 9781453746646

Publisher: Grant Perry
Editor: Michael McCullar
Project Coordinator: Robert Inks
Designer: TJ Lensing

CONTENTS

CONTENTS

AL QAEDA AND ITS FRANCHISES

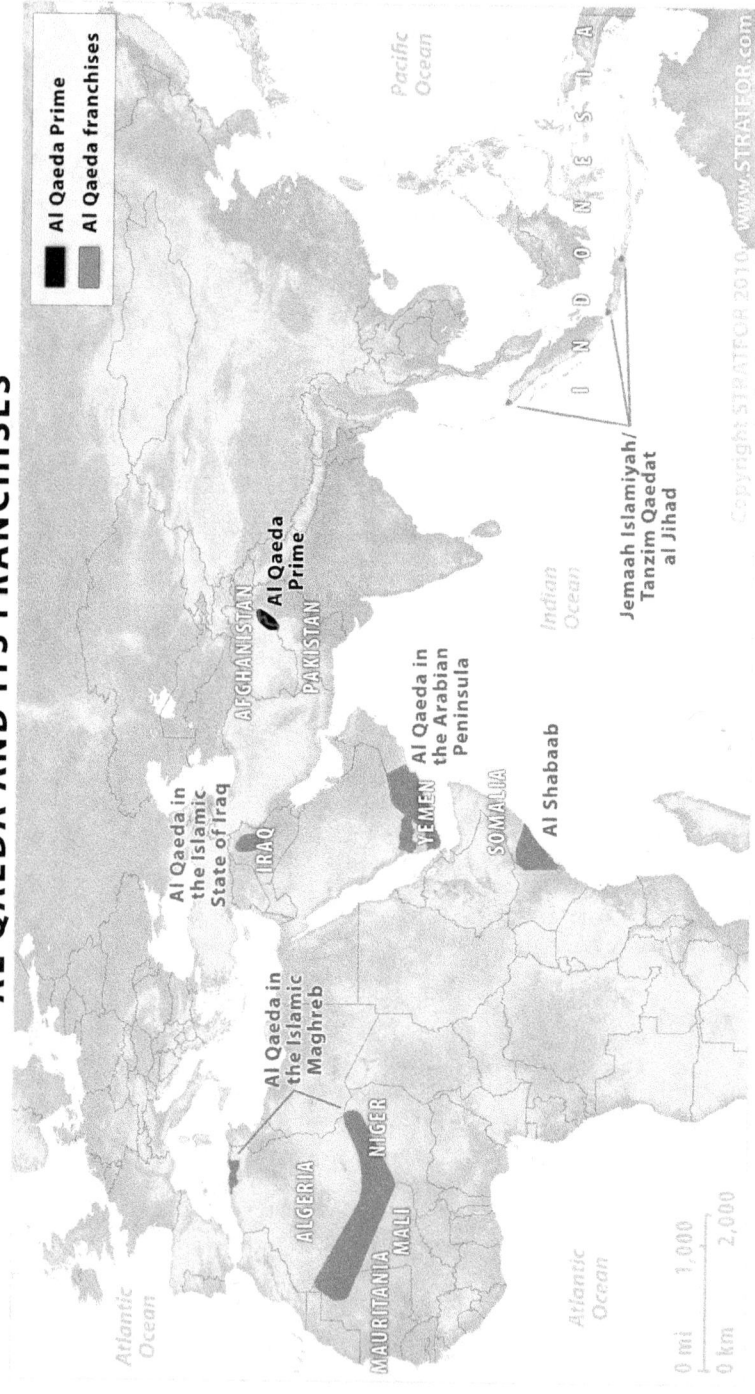

Al Qaeda Prime

Al Qaeda franchises

Al Qaeda in
the Islamic
State of Iraq

Al Qaeda
Prime

Al Qaeda in
the Arabian
Peninsula

Al Shabaab

Al Qaeda in the Islamic
Maghreb

Jemaah Islamiyah/
Tanzim Qaedat
al Jihad

AFGHANISTAN

PAKISTAN

IRAQ

YEMEN

SOMALIA

ALGERIA

MAURITANIA

MALI

NIGER

INDONESIA

Pacific
Ocean

Indian
Ocean

Atlantic
Ocean

Atlantic
Ocean

0 mi   1,000

0 km   2,000

Copyright STRATFOR 2010, www.STRATFOR.com

INTRODUCTION

Following the Sept. 11, 2001, attacks, the United States launched what it initially termed the "global war on terror" (GWOT). This offensive sought to apply the full force of all five of the levers of counterterrorism power (intelligence, military might, diplomacy, law enforcement and financial sanctions) against the global jihadist movement and its vanguard, al Qaeda. While the GWOT is now referred to as "countering violent extremism" by the Obama administration, the offensive efforts that comprised it are ongoing. For all practical purposes, the counterterrorism campaign of the Obama administration is a continuation of the campaign begun by the Bush administration.

Over time, all military organizations adapt as they adopt new technologies, change organizational doctrines and employ new tactics on the battlefield. Experience, battlefield losses and successes — and the use of new technologies and tactics by the enemy — combine to help drive these changes. Clearly, there is a big difference between the U.S. military of today and the military that fought in Vietnam. Indeed, there is even a substantial difference between how the U.S. military is equipped and operates today and how it was equipped and operated when it invaded Iraq in March 2003.

It should come as no surprise, then, that in the almost nine years that the United States and its allies have focused their counterterrorism efforts against the jihadist movement — and adjusted those efforts to make them more effective — the movement has changed and adapted in response to the pressure. This pressure has caused the al Qaeda organization — the military and ideological vanguard of the jihadist movement — to lose its sanctuary and infrastructure in Afghanistan, many of its operational leaders and a great deal of its financial support. Indeed, as an organization, al Qaeda today is a mere shell of what it was before the 9/11 attacks.

As pressure was being applied to the main al Qaeda group, regional or national militant groups in places like Iraq, the Sinai, Indonesia, Algeria and Somalia embraced the ideology of jihadism and sought to use al Qaeda's brand name as a way to attract recruits and funding to their organizations. Because of this, as the core al Qaeda group (what we refer to as al Qaeda prime) was suffering losses, these regional affiliates, or franchises, came to eclipse al Qaeda prime as the primary military threat emanating from the global jihadist movement. These franchises have generally followed a pattern where they rise up, conduct some spectacular attacks, and then get struck down. We have seen this pattern in Saudi Arabia, Indonesia and the Sinai Peninsula, and now it is seemingly being replicated in Iraq and Algeria, where the al Qaeda franchises the Islamic State of Iraq and al Qaeda in the Islamic Maghreb appear to be on the ropes. In some places, such as Egypt and Libya, these franchises have not been able to become operationally effective.

This trend toward the decentralization of jihadist military activity has continued as the leader of the al Qaeda franchise in Yemen, Nasir al-Wahayshi, has called for individual Muslims to embrace the ideology of jihadism and conduct simple attacks wherever they are. In essence, al-Wahayshi is encouraging such individuals to embrace the concept of leaderless resistance due to the heavy pressure being brought against al Qaeda prime and the franchises, pressure that has limited their ability to get jihadists to training camps in Pakistan and Yemen and has hampered their ability to conduct terrorist strikes in the West. This call for leaderless resistance was echoed by al Qaeda prime in March 2010, when Adam Gadahn, an American-born spokesman for the group, praised Ft. Hood shooter Nidal Hassan and urged his audience to follow the example of Hassan and attack targets that are close and familiar.

STRATFOR began to chronicle the decentralization of the jihadist movement in 2004, and this book is a collection of our best and most representative analyses of the topic since that time. Our forecasting and analysis has not always been well received, however, especially when our assessment has not aligned with public opinion or government analysis. For example, our assessment of the jihadist movement directly contradicted the U.S. National Intelligence Estimate published on July 17, 2007 (see page 32), and we took a great deal of heat over that fact. Time, however, has vindicated us, and our assessment of al Qaeda in 2007 was shown to be the correct one.

While such a shift toward decentralization has presented problems for counterterrorism forces, it has also proved problematic for the jihadists. For one thing, decentralized "leaderless" operatives typically lack the degree of terrorist tradecraft associated with trained terrorist operatives. This means that their plots are frequently discovered before they can be launched, or the attacks are poorly planned and executed, resulting in failed attempts.

In the final analysis, the threat posed by jihadists has been mitigated by the efforts taken against al Qaeda prime and the al Qaeda franchises. We believe they can still conduct tactical strikes and kill people, but they lack the ability at present to carry out strategically significant attacks and coordinated campaigns. However, as long as the ideology of jihadism survives, these organizations will be able to recruit new operatives and continue their struggle. This means that these organizations could regenerate if the pressure is taken off of them and they are given the opportunity to regroup and reorganize. Indeed, for the United States and its allies, the risks are many if they shift their focus away from jihadists, as they have done before.

STRATFOR
Austin, Texas
Aug. 2, 2010

A NOTE ON CONTENT

STRATFOR presents the following articles as they originally appeared on our subscription Web site, www.STRATFOR.com. These pieces represent some of our best analyses of the Islamist militant group al Qaeda since June 2004, organized under chapter headings and presented in the order in which they were published. Since most of the articles were written as individual analyses, there may be overlap from piece to piece and chapter to chapter, and some of the information may seem dated. Naturally, many of the observations herein are linked to a specific time or event that may be years removed from al Qaeda's situation today. However, STRATFOR believes bringing these pieces together provides valuable insight and perspective on a significant and historic global phenomenon.

CHAPTER 1: GOING AFTER AL QAEDA

Al Qaeda's Global Campaign: Tet Offensive or Battle of the Bulge?

July 27, 2005

A spate of attacks has occurred recently that we attribute to al Qaeda. In addition to the two rounds of attacks in London this month and the July 23 bombings at Sharm el Sheikh, Egypt, we have seen ongoing suicide bombings in Afghanistan and Iraq that targeted government officials, the bombing of a Sufi shrine in Islamabad, the abduction and murder of an Iranian security official and other killings in the Muslim world. In addition, we have seen an intensification of attacks in Iraq by Abu Musab al-Zarqawi's al Qaeda-linked faction. We are not great believers in coincidence and therefore regard these incidents as being coordinated. The degree of coordination and the method whereby coordination is achieved is murky, and not really material. But that we are experiencing an offensive by al Qaeda is clear.

At issue is the nature of the offensive. To put the matter simply, do these attacks indicate the ongoing, undiminished strength of al Qaeda, or do they represent a final, desperate counterattack — both within Iraq and globally — to attempt to reverse al Qaeda's fortunes?

In our view, the latter is the case. Al Qaeda, having been hammered over the past four years, and al-Zarqawi, facing the defection of large segments of his Sunni base of support, are engaged in a desperate attempt to reverse the course of the war. It is not clear that they will fail; such counter-offensives have succeeded in recent years. The question is whether this is a Tet Offensive or a Battle of the Bulge.

To begin to answer that, we need to consider these two offensives.

In warfare, as one side is being pressed to the point of no return, the classic maneuver is to marshal all available strength for an offensive designed to turn the tide. The offensive has a high probability of military failure and, therefore, would not be attempted until military defeat or an unacceptable political outcome appeared inevitable. The goal is to inflict a blow so striking that it throws the other side off balance. More important, it should create a crisis of confidence in the enemy's command structure and its political base. It should be a surprise attack, causing commanders to question their intelligence organizations' appreciation of the other side's condition. It should have a significant military impact. Above all, it should redefine the enemy public's perception of the course of the war. Ideally, it should set the stage for a military victory — but more probably, it would set the stage for a political settlement.

In December 1944, the Germans understood they were going to be defeated by the spring of 1945, when Soviet and Anglo-American forces would simultaneously smash into Germany. They gathered what force they had to attempt a surprise counterattack. Anglo-American intelligence organizations had concluded that the Germans were finished. The Germans took advantage of this by striking through the Ardennes Forest. Their goal was the port of Antwerp.

The fall of Antwerp — or at least, the ability to interfere with access to the port — would not have defeated the Allies. However, it would have constrained Allied offensive operations and forced postponement of the spring offensive. It also would have shaken the confidence in the Allied high command and both Roosevelt and Churchill. The unexpected nature of the offensive would have created a political crisis and opened the door to either a redefinition of Allied war aims or, possibly, a separate peace in the West.

From a military standpoint, the attack was a long shot, but not a preposterous one. Had the Germans crossed the Meuse River, they could have approached Antwerp at least. In the event, if we consider the panic that gripped the Allied high command even without the Germans reaching the Meuse, their crossing of it would have had massive repercussions. Whether it would have had political consequences is unclear. As it was, the offensive failed in the first days. It was liquidated in a matter of weeks, and the war concluded catastrophically for Germany.

A more successful example of a terminal offensive was the North Vietnamese offensive in February 1968. The Johnson administration had been arguing, with some logic, that the North Vietnamese forces were being worn down effectively by the United States, and that they were on the defensive and declining. The Tet Offensive was intended to reverse the waning fortunes of the North Vietnamese. There were a number of goals. First and foremost, the offensive was designed to demonstrate to all parties that the North Vietnamese retained a massive offensive capability. It was intended to drive a wedge between U.S. commanders in Saigon and political leaders in Washington by demonstrating that the Saigon command was providing misleading analysis. Finally, it was intended to drive a wedge between the Johnson administration and the American public.

From a strictly military standpoint, Tet was a complete disaster. It squandered scarce resources on an offensive that neither reduced U.S. strength nor gained and held strategic objectives. After the offensive was over, the North Vietnamese army was back where it had started, with far fewer troops and supplies.

From the political point of view, however, it was wildly successful. A chasm opened between the civilian leadership in Washington and Gen. William Westmoreland in Saigon. Westmoreland's rejection of intelligence analyses pointing to an offensive undermined confidence in him. Far more important, Johnson's speeches about lights at the end of the tunnel lost all credibility, in spite of the fact that he wasn't altogether wrong. The apparent success of the Tet Offensive forced a re-evaluation of American strategy in Vietnam, Johnson's decision not to stand for re-election and a general sense that the U.S. government had vastly underestimated the strength and tenacity of the North Vietnamese.

Declining military fortunes force combatants to consider political solutions. At that point, military action becomes focused on three things:

- Demonstrating to all concerned that you retain effective offensive capabilities.

- Convincing the enemy that a military solution is impossible.

- Creating a political atmosphere in which negotiations and/or military victory are possible.

In their Ardennes offensive in 1944, the Germans failed in the first goal and therefore could not achieve the others. In the case of the Tet Offensive, Americans became convinced that the North Vietnamese could still mount offensives, could not be defeated and therefore had to be negotiated with. The negotiations and truce bought the North Vietnamese time to regroup, reinforce and bring the war to a satisfactory solution (from their standpoint).

Vietnam's guerrilla warfare bears little resemblance to the massed, combined arms conflict in World War II. Neither even slightly reflects the global covert offensive mounted by al Qaeda, nor the asymmetric response of the United States. Nevertheless, all wars share common characteristics:

- A political object — for example, domination of Europe, unification of Vietnam, creation of radical Islamist states in the Muslim world.

- All use the military means at hand to achieve these goals.

- In all wars, one side or the other reaches a point beyond which there is only defeat. That point calls for the final offensive to be launched.

- The offensive is not hopeless, but its ends are primarily political rather than military. Its goal is to redefine the enemy's psychology as well as bolster the spirits of one's own forces.

The key to success, at that point, is two-fold. First, the offensive must appear to be an ongoing operation. It cannot appear to be a hastily contrived, desperation move. The Germans didn't succeed in this at the Battle of the Bulge. The North Vietnamese did at Tet. Second, the offensive must have the desired psychological effect: It must reverse the enemy's expectation of victory. The claims by civil and military leaders on the other side that the war is under control must be discredited.

It has been our view for months that the United States is winning — not has won — the U.S.-jihadist war. Events in the recent past have reinforced our view. In Iraq, for example, the decision by a large segment of the Sunni leadership to join in the political process has posed a mortal challenge to the jihadists. They depend on the Sunni community to provide sanctuary, recruits and supplies. If any large segment of the Sunni community abandons them, their ability to wage war — on the scale it is currently being waged — is undermined. They will, however, be able to sustain a much smaller and less politically significant scale of operations.

In the broader, global fight, al Qaeda continues to face this reality. There has not been a single revolution overthrowing a Muslim government in favor of a radical/militant Islamist regime. In fact, the bulk of the Muslim states are actively cooperating with the United States. The primary intent of the radical and militant Islamists, which is to create a caliphate based on at least one significant Muslim state, has been completely thwarted. This point has not been missed in the Islamic world.

At this point, al Qaeda needs to launch a counteroffensive on a global scale that is designed to demonstrate its viability as a paramilitary force. People tend to denigrate the complexity of terrorist operations. This complexity is not in the willingness to blow oneself up but in the acquisition of explosives, the transmitting of messages internationally and the ability to go about undetected. The 9/11 attacks were a superbly executed operation. Al Qaeda has set a standard of credibility for itself, and to create the reversal of fortunes it requires, it must carry out an operation on that order.

Yet since the Sept. 11 attacks, the scale of al Qaeda's operations outside the Islamic world has declined. Al Qaeda badly needs to re-establish its credibility and recapture its earlier momentum by mounting an attack on the scale of 9/11 or beyond. There is no need to delay and every incentive to move as quickly as possible. Al Qaeda needs this for political reasons and also because the pressure from national intelligence agencies is such that to wait is to risk losing the operational team (if one is ready to strike). If al Qaeda has a nuclear weapon, for example, the longer it waits to use it, the more likely it is to be captured in transit to its target. The pressure is on for al Qaeda to act as quickly and as effectively as it can.

The London attacks were a failure. It's not only that the Tube attacks lacked the ferocity of 9/11. However tragic the loss of life, the first attack was a work of mediocre effectiveness, while the 7/21 attempt was a joke. The attacks elsewhere, particularly at Sharm el Sheikh, were more effective but still didn't rise to the levels required to establish credibility.

What al Qaeda has demonstrated is that its available assets, particularly outside the Islamic world, lack the skill and sophistication to come close even to the level of the Madrid attacks, let alone those in New York. Their attempt to increase the tempo of operations has led al Qaeda to use untrained and unsuitable personnel. It has not achieved the psychological ends it wishes.

Al Qaeda has one hope. If the ability to mount modest terrorist operations with increased frequency convinces its enemies that it is more viable than was thought, at that point it will begin to be successful. That perception will transfer to the Muslim world and, with it, al Qaeda could recover the credibility it needs to continue to wage war. At the moment, however, that doesn't seem to be happening. The major political result of London, for example, has been a tendency among Muslim leaders to condemn the attacks in numbers and vehemence rarely seen before. Al Qaeda's glory days seem to be behind it. Which means that al Qaeda must up the ante if it can. We do not believe it will be able to do so. More precisely, if it had the ability, there have been so many other moments to have acted that it seems odd that it didn't. We also doubt that al Qaeda has recently acquired the means to attack. It is under heavy pressure, and it is harder now for it to grow than it was before. There are al Qaeda sympathizers, but al Qaeda has maintained its internal security by not growing. It is relying on untrained sympathizers to carry out missions. It is hard to believe that al Qaeda has much left in its kit.

Still, the outcome of any last-ditch offensive is uncertain. The very fact that it is happening can panic enemy forces or drive a wedge between the government and the military, and between the government and the public. Bush's popularity is slipping, and the perception that al Qaeda is waging a successful and unstoppable offensive could suddenly undermine his position. He is vulnerable at the moment. But, thus far, the attempt at a global Tet Offensive has failed to rise to the level of credibility required. Al Qaeda must do something of substantial significance before the summer ends, or see its position in Iraq and in other places deteriorate rapidly.

As with the Germans and Vietnamese, al Qaeda's time of mortal crisis is its time of maximum available effort. We doubt that it can pull this off, but we will wait until September to see.

Attacking into the Pyramid
July 28, 2005

"In a July 25 report titled Al Qaeda's Global Campaign: Tet Offensive or Battle of the Bulge?" (see page 1), we proposed that al Qaeda is engaging in the terrorist equivalent of a Tet Offensive: launching a series of attacks — some significant, others mere psyops — in an effort to turn the tide of a war it has been losing. Certainly, there is evidence of such a shift at the strategic level, in terms of the number and pace of operations around the globe, but at the tactical level there appears to be a widespread case of business as usual.

Let's take a moment to examine that statement. Al Qaeda has taken some heavy hits in the past few years, losing a number of high-value operatives — planners and tacticians such as Khalid Sheikh Mohammed, Hambali, Abu Farj al-Libi and Mohammad Naeem Noor Khan. This likely has contributed, at least in part, to perceptions that it is losing its edge — turning to poorly trained local sympathizers to carry out attacks, such as the July 7 bombings in London, or the more recent series of explosions in Sharm el-Sheikh, Egypt.

The truth of the matter, however, is that this is how al Qaeda has operated throughout its history — with the notable exception of the Sept. 11 strikes. The July 7 attacks in London were jarring to Westerners because most of the suicide bombers were British-born citizens attacking on their home soil. In fact, most al Qaeda attacks — ranging from the 1998 embassy bombings in East Africa to the Khobar Towers attacks to the 1993 World Trade Center strike to the Bali nightclubs — have been carried out by locals, with the help of an al Qaeda operational leader.

Woven throughout this history of deadly successes are a series of equally notable, and at times almost laughable, failures, such that even the aborted July 21 attacks against the Tube in London don't really seem surprising. At one point, for example, the storied Abdel Basit (aka Ramzi Yousef) and his assistant Abdul Hakim Murad caught themselves on fire in Manila while cooking a batch of triacetone triperoxide. A fair number of 20-watt actors — with names like Ahmad Ajaj, Richard Reid and Ahmed Ressam — who rendered themselves ineffective through bumbling have always been part of the group.

At the tactical level, we are seeing a shift (and with good reason) away from the elaborate, grandiose killing schemes that characterized 9/11 and various precursor plots, such as Operation Bojinka, in favor of the simple and utilitarian — if still coordinated — strike. As a rule, al Qaeda planners seem to have adopted the maxim that "less is more."

The loss of what might be called tactical sophistication, however, does not necessarily mean that al Qaeda is now gasping its last as an organization. The Tet-like offensive, obviously, is meant to help the group regain credibility and some of its earlier momentum, which eventually could lead to growth or regeneration. But even if it fails in that effort, the current trend — should it hold — points toward a fundamental intelligence problem and a crucial shift in the way the war against al Qaeda is fought, rather than the end of fighting itself.

For purposes of this discussion, it is useful to think of al Qaeda in terms of a pyramid. The apex of its leadership — Osama bin Laden, Ayman al-Zawahiri and others known to the world through video clips — are on the run, believed to be hiding in Pakistan or adjacent areas of southwest Asia. The middle layer is populated by tactical commanders, couriers and logistical planners — connected, knowledgeable, well-trained and high-value operatives who, logic argues, must be small in number in order to maintain operational security for the group. It is this layer that has been heavily targeted by covert intelligence and security agencies, for obvious reasons: These operatives are the key to reducing both the numbers of attacks and the worst of the carnage.

At the bottom of the pyramid are al Qaeda's foot soldiers. These are local sympathizers and militants with rudimentary training, those who waste themselves in suicide attacks or can be cut loose if arrested and questioned, with little impact to the rest of the organization. This is a finite but still significant sea of potential suspects, through which move the likes of Mohammed Sidique Khan — the apparent ringleader of the July 7 suicide cell — who may have attracted the notice of authorities in the past, but then been dismissed as a potential threat. It also likely is home to others who live completely below the radar — nameless, to the wider world, until after the bombs detonate.

Judging from the types and relative simplicity of the attacks now being carried out, we can theorize that a certain amount of attrition has occurred within al Qaeda's middle command tier. The impact of that attrition is perhaps best illustrated by the al-Hindi takedown — part of a larger rollup of al Qaeda operatives that triggered a heightened security alert on the East Coast of the United States last year.

Dhiren Barot, better known by his nom de guerre Abu Eisa al-Hindi, is believed to have been a regional militant commander operating out of Britain and probably the United States. Between August 2000 and April 2001, al-Hindi is believed to have conducted surveillance on several landmarks in New York City, Newark, N.J., and Washington, D.C. — including the world headquarters of the International Monetary Fund and the World Bank, Prudential Corporate Plaza, the New York Stock Exchange and Citigroup Centre. Authorities discovered evidence of very serious engineering-type surveillance focusing on the design of the buildings. This is suited for one purpose — to bring them down.

An al-Hindi — the likes of whom populate the middle tier of the pyramid — is very unlikely to be found taking part in the actual operations of a plot, but instead would transmit plans and instructions through a field command to the foot soldiers who carry out attacks. Had the plans he was helping to foment been carried out, the economic and psychological impact would have been quite serious — perhaps rivaling that of 9/11.

Contrast that, then, with the Tube attacks in London. In the 7/7 attacks, the bombers committed a number of easily avoided violations of operational security — including carrying their own identification documents — struck at poorly defended ("soft") targets, and detonated their explosives in ways that, while deadly, did not inflict the greatest damage or loss of life possible under the circumstances.

From these examples and others, it appears that al Qaeda has suffered a rather serious decline in the quality — though not necessarily the quantity — of its operational assets, which in turn points toward a decline in its effectiveness as a strategic force wielding influence over world events (though not, on the whole, as an organization capable of violence). On a related note, it also appears that national intelligence and security agencies in the United States and elsewhere who have taken "preventing the next 9/11" as their primary mission have been successful, at least so far.

But herein lies the problem. The middle layer of the pyramid — that consisting of highly skilled operatives — might be seriously damaged, but it has not yet been eliminated. We strongly suspect the existence of an al Qaeda "ghost" — a high-value operative, likely someone with dual nationality or multiple passports — who is still able to move from cell to cell or at least transmit signals to local groups awaiting a "go" order to carry out a strike. Government-run intelligence agencies have suspected the same, and MI5 actually identified a possible ghost, named on a terrorism watch list, who entered and left Britain shortly before the July 7 attacks. Yet the agency also signaled, three weeks prior to the event, that there were "no known threats" to world leaders who would be attending the G-8 summit in Scotland at that time. Clearly, the intelligence puzzle is not yet complete.

The intelligence dilemmas and failures are magnified at the foot-soldier level. Again, using the London case as an example, consider that Khan and possibly other members of his cell had been investigated — and then dismissed as potential threats — prior to the attacks. This analysis might have been wrong on its face or utterly correct at the time — but the threat is no more static than human beings themselves.

At its simplest level, the dilemma is mathematical: There are too many potential targets, which cost too much to fully defend, with too few government resources, against too large a universe of potential actors — the bottom tier of the pyramid. Without significant help from human intelligence sources — and a great deal of luck — it is all but impossible to prevent some forms of terrorist attack (exemplified by London). The best any government intelligence or security force can do is to defend the highest-value targets and take pains to mitigate, rather than prevent, the damage or loss of life elsewhere.

Intelligence failures occur for a variety of reasons but almost always boil down to a lack of tactical analysis, lack of human intelligence needed to develop sufficient detail to thwart an attack, and failure to identify and penetrate terrorist cells — again, due to a dearth of actionable information.

National and international security agencies can be expected to continue focusing efforts against the high-value ghosts who haunt the middle tier of al Qaeda's structure, but even a complete rupture of strategic communications between the apex and bottom tier of the pyramid would not, in our view, put an end to the wider war at the tactical level. For that, the key is going to be nothing more — and nothing less — than old-fashioned cooperation and human intelligence at the grassroots level.

Four Years on: Who is Winning the War, and How Can Anyone Tell?
Sept. 14, 2005

Four years have passed since al Qaeda attacked the United States. It is difficult to remember a war of which the status has been more difficult to assess. Indeed, there are reasonable people who argue that the conflict between the United States and al Qaeda is not a war at all, and that thinking of it in those terms obscures reality. Other reasonable people argue that it is only in thinking in terms of war that the conflict makes sense — and these people can be divided into two groups: those who believe the United States is winning the war and those who believe it is losing it. Into this confusion we must add the question of whether the Iraq war is part of what U.S. President George W. Bush refers to as the "war on terrorism" and what others might call the war against al Qaeda. Even the issues are not clear. It is a war in which no one can agree even on the criteria for success or failure or, at times, who is on what side.

Part of this dilemma is simply the result of partisan politics. It is a myth that Americans unite in times of war: Anyone who believes they do must read the history of, for example, the Mexican War.

Americans are a fractious people and, while they were united during World War II, the political recriminations were only delayed — not suspended. The issue here is not partisanship, however, but rather that there is no clear framework against which to judge the current war.

Let us begin with what we all — save for those who believe that the Sept. 11 attacks were a plot hatched by the U.S. government to justify the PATRIOT Act — can agree on:

- Al Qaeda attacked the United States on Sept. 11, 2001, by hijacking aircraft and crashing or trying to crash them into well-known buildings.

- Since Sept. 11, there have been al Qaeda attacks in Europe and several Muslim countries, but not in the United States.

- The United States invaded Afghanistan a month after the strikes against the World Trade Center and the Pentagon, forcing the Taliban out of the major cities but not defeating them. The United States has failed to capture Osama bin Laden, although it has captured other key al Qaeda operatives. The Taliban have regrouped and are now conducting an insurgency in Afghanistan.

- The United States invaded Iraq in 2003. The Bush administration claimed that this was part of the war against al Qaeda; critics have claimed it had nothing to do with the war.

- The United States failed to win the Iraq war rapidly, as it had expected to do. Instead, U.S. forces encountered a difficult guerrilla war that, while confined generally to the Sunni regions, nevertheless posed serious military and political challenges.

- Al Qaeda has failed to achieve its primary political goal — that is, to trigger an uprising in at least one major Muslim country and create a jihadist regime. There has been no general rising in the Muslim world, and most governments are now cooperating with the United States.

13

- There have been no follow-on attacks in the United States since Sept. 11. Whether this is because al Qaeda had no plans for a second attack or because subsequent attacks were disrupted by U.S. intelligence is not clear.

This is not intended to be an exhaustive list, but rather to provide what we would regard as a non-controversial base from which to proceed with an assessment.

From the beginning, then, it has been unclear whether the United States saw itself as fighting a war against al Qaeda or as carrying out a criminal investigation. The two are, of course, enormously different. This is a critical problem.

The administration's use of the term "war on terrorism" began the confusion. Terrorism is a mode of warfare. Save for those instances when lunatics like Timothy McVeigh use it as an end in itself, terrorism is a method of intimidating the civilian population in order to drive a wedge between the public and their government. Al Qaeda, then, had a political purpose in using terrorism, as did the British in their nighttime bombing of Germany or the Germans in their air raids against London. The problem in the Bush administration's use of this term is that you do not wage a war against a method of warfare. A war is waged against an enemy force.

Now, there are those who argue that war is something that takes place between nation-states and that al Qaeda, not being a nation-state, is not waging war. We tend to disagree with this view. Al Qaeda is not a nation-state, but it was a coherent, disciplined force using violence for political ends. The United States, by focusing on the "war on terror," confused the issue endlessly. But the critics of the war, who insisted that wartime measures were unnecessary because this was not a war, compounded the confusion. By the time we were done, the "war on terror" had extended itself to include campaigns against animal rights groups, and attempts to prevent terror attacks were seen as violations of human rights by the ACLU.

It is odd to raise these points at the beginning of an analysis of a war, but no war can be fought when there isn't even clarity about

14

what it is you are doing, let alone who you are fighting. Yet that is precisely how this war evolved, and then degenerated into conceptual chaos. The whole issue also got bound up with internal name-calling, to the point that any assertion that Bush had some idea of what he was doing was seen as outrageous partisanship, and the assertion that Bush was failing in what he was doing was viewed the same way. Where there is no clarity, there can be no criteria for success or failure. That is the crisis today. No one agrees as to what is happening; therefore, no one can explain who is winning or losing.

Out of this situation came the deeper confusion: Iraq. From the beginning, it was not clear why the United States invaded Iraq. The Bush administration offered three explanations: First, that there were weapons of mass destruction in Iraq; second, that Iraq was complicit with al Qaeda; and finally, that a democratic Iraq — and creation of a democratic Muslim world — would help stop terrorism (or, more precisely, al Qaeda).

The three explanations were untenable on their face. Contrary to myth, the Bush administration did not rush to go to war in Iraq. The administration had been talking about it for nearly a year before the invasion began. That would not have been the case if there truly was a fear that the Iraqis might be capable of building atomic bombs, since they might hurry up and build them. You don't give a heads-up in that situation. The United States did. Hence, it wasn't about WMD. Second, it wasn't about Iraq's terrorist ties. Saddam Hussein had no problem with the concept of terrorism, but he was an ideological enemy of everything bin Laden stood for. Hussein was a secular militarist; bin Laden, a religious ideologue. Cooperation between them wasn't likely, and pointing to obscure meetings that Mohammed Atta may or may not have had with an Iraqi in Prague didn't make the case. Finally, the democracy explanation came late in the game. Bush had campaigned against nation-building in places like Kosovo — and if he now believed in nation-building as a justification for war, it meant he stood with Bill Clinton. He dodged that criticism, though, because the media couldn't remember Kosovo or spell it anymore by the time Iraq rolled around.

Bush's enemies argued that he invaded Iraq in order to (a) avenge the fact that Hussein had tried to kill his father; (b) as part of a long-term strategy planned years before to dominate the Middle East; (c) to dominate all of the oil in Iraq; (d) because he was a bad man; or (e) just because. The fact was that his critics had no idea why he did it and generated fantastic theories because they couldn't figure it out any more than Bush could explain it.

STRATFOR readers know our view was that the invasion of Iraq was intended to serve three purposes:

- To bring pressure on the Saudi government, which was allowing Saudis to funnel money to al Qaeda, to halt this enablement and to cooperate with U.S. intelligence. The presence of U.S. troops to the north of Saudi Arabia was intended to drive home the seriousness of the situation.

- To take control of the most strategic country in the Middle East — Iraq borders seven critical countries — and to use it as a base of operations against other countries that were cooperating with al Qaeda.

- To demonstrate in the Muslim world that the American reputation for weakness and indecisiveness — well-earned in the two decades prior to the Sept. 11 attacks — was no longer valid. The United States was aware that the invasion of Iraq would enrage the Muslim world but banked on it frightening it as well.

Let's put it this way: The key to understanding the situation was that Bush wanted to blackmail the Saudis, use Iraq as a military base and terrify Muslims. He wanted to do this, but he did not want to admit this was what he was doing. He therefore provided implausible justifications, operating under the theory that a rapid victory brushes aside troubling questions. Clinton had gotten out of Kosovo without explaining why signs of genocide were never found, because the war was over quickly and everyone was sick of it. Bush figured he would do the same thing in Iraq.

It was precisely at this point that the situation got out of control. The biggest intelligence failure of the United States was not 9/11 — only Monday morning quarterbacks can claim that they would have spotted al Qaeda's plot and been able to block it. Nor was it the failure to find WMD in Iraq. Not only was that not the point, but actually, everyone was certain that Hussein at least had chemical weapons. Even the French believed he did. The biggest mistake was the intelligence that said that the Iraqis wouldn't fight, that U.S. forces would be welcomed or at least not greeted hostilely by the Iraqi public, and that the end of conventional combat would end the war.

That was the really significant intelligence failure. Hussein, or at least some of his key commanders, knew perfectly well that the United States would crush their conventional forces, so they created the material and financial basis for a protracted guerrilla war. U.S. intelligence did not see this coming, and thus had not prepared the U.S. force for fighting the guerrilla war. Indeed, if they had known this was coming, Bush might well have calculated differently on invading Iraq — since he wasn't going to get the decisive victory he needed.

The intelligence failure was compounded by a command failure. By mid-April 2003, it was evident to STRATFOR that a guerrilla war was starting. Donald Rumsfeld continued vigorously to deny that any such war was going on. It was not until July, when Gen. Tommy Franks was relieved by John Abizaid as Central Command chief, that the United States admitted the obvious. Those were the 45-60 critical days. Intelligence failures happen in every war, worse than this one, but the delay in recognizing what was happening — the extended denial in the Pentagon — eliminated any chance of nipping it in the bud. By the summer of 2003, the war was raging, and foreign jihadists had begun joining in. Obviously, this increased anti-American sentiment, but not necessarily effective anti-American sentiment. Hating the United States is not the same as being able to run secure covert operations in the United States.

The war did not and does not cover most of Iraq's territory. Only a relatively small portion is involved — the Sunni regions. At this point, the administration has done a fairly good job in creating a political process and bringing the Sunni elders to the table, if not to an agreement that will end the insurgency. But the problem is that American expectations about the war have been so strangely set that whatever esoteric satisfaction experts might take in the evolution, it is clear that this war is not what the Bush administration expected, that it is not what the administration was prepared to fight, and that the administration is now in a position where it has to make compromises rather than impose its will.

We believe that a war started on Sept. 11, 2001. We believe that from a strictly operational point of view, al Qaeda has gotten by far the worst of it. Having struck the first blow, al Qaeda has been crippled, with each succeeding attack weaker and weaker. We also think that the U.S. invasion of Iraq achieved at least one of Washington's goals: Saudi Arabia has behaved much differently since February 2003. But the ongoing war has undermined the ability of the United States to use Iraq as a base of operations in the region, and the psychological outcome Washington was hoping for obviously didn't materialize.

What progress there has been is invisible, for two reasons. First, the Bush administration had crafted an explanation for the entire war that was based on two premises — that the American public would remain united on all measures necessary after Sept. 11 and that the United States would achieve a quick victory in Iraq, sparing the administration the need to explain itself. As a result, Bush has never articulated a coherent strategic position. Furthermore, as the second premise proved untrue, the failure to enunciate a coherent strategic vision began to undermine the first premise — national unity. At this point, Bush is beginning to face criticism in his own party. Sen. Chuck Hagel's statement, that the promise to stay the course does not constitute a strategy, is indicative of Bush's major problem.

The president's dilemma, now, is this. He had a strategy. He failed to explain what it was because doing so would have carried a cost, and the president assumed it was unnecessary. It turned out to be necessary, but he still didn't enunciate a strategy because it would at that point have appeared contrived. Moreover, as time went on, the strategy had to evolve. It is hard to evolve an unarticulated strategy. Bush rigidified publicly even as his strategy in Iraq became more nimble.

Figuring out how the war is going four years after 9/11, then, is like a nightmare fighting ghosts. The preposterous defense of U.S. strategy meets the preposterous attack on U.S. strategy: Claims that the United States invaded Iraq to bring democracy to the people compete with the idea that it invaded in order to give contracts to Halliburton. Nothing is too preposterous to claim.

But even as U.S. politics seize up in one of these periodic spasms, these facts are still clear:

- The United States has not been attacked in four years.
- No Muslim government has fallen to supporters of al Qaeda.
- The United States has won in neither Iraq nor Afghanistan.
- Bin Laden is still free and ready to go extra rounds.

So far, neither side has won — but on the whole, we'd say the United States has the edge. The war is being fought outside the United States. And that is not a trivial point. But it is not yet a solution to the president's problems.

The Quiet Campaign Against Al Qaeda's Local Nodes
June 20, 2007

Indonesian authorities announced June 15 that they had arrested Zarkasih, the acting head of Jemaah Islamiyah (JI), an al Qaeda-linked militant group that has conducted several major attacks in Indonesia. Zarkasih, who succeeded Abu Bakar Bashir and Abu Rusdan as JI leader, was captured June 9 in the same operation that netted another top JI leader, Abu Dujana, an operative trained by al Qaeda in Afghanistan who headed the group's military wing.

The capture of these two major figures alone would be a significant blow to JI. However, when they are combined with the steady stream of other JI leaders who have been killed or captured since JI carried out its most devastating attack — the October 2002 bombings in Bali that killed more than 200 people — the impact becomes even more significant. In other words, few of the leaders remain who directed JI up to and including the 2002 attacks.

The Indonesian government's campaign against JI, part of the "global war on terror," has been bolstered by assistance from the United States, Australia and other Western nations. Moreover, the fight against JI is not confined to Indonesia itself but is a regional effort involving other governments in Southeast Asia. These efforts have kept JI off balance and unable to launch a major attack since the October 2005 suicide bombings in Bali. The Indonesian government also has been able to seize large quantities of weapons and explosives — ordnance that no longer can be used in terrorist attacks.

The success against JI underscores one important fact: Although much of the world's attention regarding the war on terrorism — which really is a war against jihadists — has been focused on Iraq and to a lesser extent Afghanistan, a quiet and quite successful campaign is being waged against the local nodes, those regional or national militant groups supporting al Qaeda in places like Indonesia, Saudi Arabia, Egypt and North Africa. The war on jihadism, however, is at its heart an ideological war, and as long as the ideology of jihadism survives, these regional nodes — and al Qaeda itself — cannot be eradicated.

The Local Nodes

Al Qaeda's leaders have always known that al Qaeda, as an organization, lacks the strength to achieve its goals of ending infidel influence in Muslim lands and overthrowing the "corrupt" regimes ruling them. Because of this, al Qaeda has viewed itself as a "vanguard organization" and, as such, aims to serve as an example for the larger Muslim community (or ummah) to follow and to convince the ummah to join the jihad (or its definition of jihad). Al Qaeda's hope is that its example will lead to a global uprising among the ummah and that this "awakened" community will wield the force necessary to achieve jihadist objectives.

This context helps to explain the relationships al Qaeda's leaders have fostered with local groups in such places as Indonesia, Afghanistan, Algeria and Iraq. They believe these local or regional organizations are important partners that provide a bridge for the transfer of their ideology to the ummah in the various regions where they operate. Many, indeed most, of the thousands of fighters al Qaeda has trained over the years in camps in Sudan, Afghanistan, Pakistan and elsewhere were not al Qaeda members per se, but rather men like Dujana who would return home and join regional groups like JI, or others who would go back and form grassroots cells, like Mohammed Sidique Khan, who established the cell that conducted the July 7, 2005, London bombings.

Al Qaeda's attention to local jihadist groups, therefore, clearly is not the result of the group's difficulties following the U.S. invasion of Afghanistan. In fact, al Qaeda leader Osama bin Laden has always placed emphasis on working with these groups. For example, in February 1998, when bin Laden announced the formation of what he called the "World Islamic Front," the organization's fatwa calling for "jihad against Jews and crusaders" was also signed by Ayman al-Zawahiri, who at the time led a faction of the Egyptian Islamic Jihad (EIJ) group; Rifai Ahmad Taha, leader of his faction of the Egyptian Gamaah al-Islamiyah (GAI); Shaykh Mir Hamzah, secretary of his faction of the Jamiat-ul-Ulema-e-Pakistan; and Fazlul Rahman, leader of the Jihad Movement in Bangladesh.

Al-Zawahiri's EIJ was one of the first of these regional or local groups to officially join forces with bin Laden and al Qaeda, though when that union took place, EIJ had splintered and its new militant wing had suffered major setbacks. The militant faction under al-Zawahiri not only had been largely decimated inside Egypt, but U.S.-led operations also had resulted in the capture or death of many of its senior operatives outside of Egypt in such places as Albania and Kuwait.

Although many of these local groups received training from al Qaeda and worked closely with it, for the most part they maintained their independence. During the 1990s, for example, GAI members were trained at al Qaeda facilities in Sudan and Afghanistan, and some, including GAI leader Mustafa Hamza, even worked for businesses bin Laden owned in Sudan. Furthermore, bin Laden and al Qaeda helped organize and fund GAI and EIJ's cooperative attempt to assassinate Egyptian President Hosni Mubarak in Addis Ababa in 1995.

When GAI fractured in the late 1990s and the bulk of the group denounced violence and jihadism, Taha, the militant faction's leader, maintained close relations with al Qaeda. He even appeared alongside bin Laden and al-Zawahiri in a September 2000 video calling for the release of GAI spiritual leader Sheikh Omar Abdel-Rahman, who was (and is) in a U.S. prison. Abdel-Rahman was convicted in October 1995 on charges of seditious conspiracy for, among other things, issuing a verbal fatwa that condoned a plan to attack several targets in New York, saying the plan was permissible under Islam. However, in spite of the close relationship, GAI's militant faction did not announce its merger with al Qaeda until August 2006.

The Rush to Join the Caravan

Though the 9/11 attacks did not spark the widespread uprising of the ummah al Qaeda was hoping for, the spectacular success of the attacks made bin Laden a household name and vaulted al Qaeda into the media spotlight. Despite the Taliban's quick overthrow in Afghanistan, which resulted in the scattering of al Qaeda and the relocation of its leadership to Pakistan's North-West Frontier Province, al Qaeda continued to be perceived as the apex of the jihadist movement in the Western media and, perhaps more important, on the streets of the Muslim world.

Following the aggressive action of the U.S. government and its allies against jihadist groups in the wake of the 9/11 attacks, many people who previously praised bin Laden and al Qaeda renounced the group's tactics, including GAI leader Hamza. However, in October 2004, the leader of a little-known jihadist group in Iraq, Jamaat al-Tawhid and Jihad (Monotheism and Jihad), changed the name of his group to Tandheem al Qaeda fi Bilad al-Rafidain (al Qaeda Organization in the Land of the Two Rivers) and swore allegiance to bin Laden. In a December 2004 statement, bin Laden confirmed this alliance, referring to the leader of that group, Abu Musab al-Zarqawi, as the "leader of al Qaeda in Iraq."

This move by al-Zarqawi was hugely successful. By associating his network with al Qaeda, al-Zarqawi made it prominent among the many jihadist and nationalist insurgent groups operating in Iraq — and quickly achieved name-brand recognition. This recognition rapidly translated into an influx of fighters, both foreign and Iraqi, for the group and a much-needed infusion of capital. In fact, al-Zarqawi's organization was so flush with cash that in a July 2005 letter, al-Zawahiri asks al-Zarqawi to send financial assistance.

Within a short period of time, al-Zarqawi's group became one of the pre-eminent militant groups in Iraq. Al-Zarqawi himself became a household name since his group posted frequent statements and videos of its operations against coalition and Iraqi forces on the Internet. In some ways, al-Zarqawi had even surpassed bin Laden in terms of media coverage and notoriety.

Though al-Zarqawi's meteoric rise was cut short by his death in a June 2006 airstrike, the success he enjoyed by adopting the al Qaeda brand was not missed by other interested observers. In August 2006, the militant wing of the Egyptian GAI released a video announcing it had formally joined al Qaeda. Three months later, Algeria's Salafist Group for Preaching and Combat (GSPC) announced that it was forming a unified command with Morocco's Islamic Combatant Group, Libya's Islamic Fighting Group and several Tunisian groups. The new group was to be called the al Qaeda Organization for the Countries of the Arab Maghreb.

Kashmiri Islamist militant groups also are now attempting to jump on this bandwagon, as demonstrated by the "Declaration of War against India" they issued in the name of al Qaeda earlier in June.

Status of the Nodes

To date, none of these newer local nodes has realized the same level of success that al-Zarqawi's group did. The Egyptian node has carried out no successful attacks since its highly publicized announcement. The Moroccan element of the new Maghreb al Qaeda node apparently attempted to go operational in March and April but its poor tactics and inadequate planning resulted in the death of more suicide bombers than targets.

Perhaps the most successful of these new groups is the Algerian element of the Maghreb al Qaeda node, the former GSPC. The Algerian group has conducted several attacks, including an April 11 double suicide attack involving vehicle-borne improvised explosive devices. Those bombs struck the prime minister's office and a police station in Algiers. The Algerian government, however, has cracked down on the group and its supporters since those attacks.

In many ways, the Algerian group seems to be following a trajectory previously seen elsewhere, in which a local node emerges, conducts some successful attacks and then is hit hard by local authorities (often with assistance from U.S. intelligence and law enforcement agencies.) This is essentially what has happened to some of the older nodes, such as JI in Indonesia, Egypt's Tawhid wa al-Jihad in Sinai, and the Saudi al Qaeda node. There were signs in January of a possible revival of the Saudi node, but other than a simple shooting attack in late February — followed by a major hit against the group by Saudi authorities — the node has been quiet.

Even al-Zarqawi's node, which undertook several operations in Jordan before his death, including the November 2005 Amman hotel bombings, has been unable to project its power outside of Iraq as of late. This node also has been receiving pressure from elements in Iraq and has started to fight Iraqi nationalists. If a political settlement is reached between the United States and Iran regarding Iraq, this node could quickly find itself unwelcome in Iraq — and even more embattled.

The Future

Given that most of the al Qaeda local nodes currently are doing poorly, and those that are doing fairly well now could be looking at bleak futures, does that mean they pose no threat? Absolutely not.

Though the campaign to disrupt the local nodes — the war against jihadism — has been very successful, it is important to remember that this is not so much a war against a group of individuals as it is a war against an ideology. The problem is, ideologies are harder to kill than people. Consider, for example, how the revolutionary ideas of Karl Marx, Vladimir Lenin and Che Guevara have outlived the men themselves.

In the same way, the al Qaeda ideology will outlast bin Laden, as the call to jihad outlasted bin Laden's friend and mentor, Abdullah Azzam. So even if bin Laden were to be eliminated next week, the struggle would continue. The nodes may be disorganized and their operations disrupted, but as long as they can recruit new fighters and raise money, they will retain the ability to reorganize and carry out attacks. The key, therefore, will be in undermining the ideology of jihadism and thereby cutting into the jihadist recruiting pool and drying up its funding.

The problem for the United States is that it cannot fight this ideological war, and any efforts it openly supports — including the Arabic television station Al Hurra — are quickly tainted and discredited. The U.S. government, therefore, must sit on the sidelines while moderate Muslim scholars refute the theology of jihadism and hope the message gets through.

Gunning for Al Qaeda Prime
June 27, 2007

Al Qaeda's media branch, As-Sahab, released a statement by Ayman al-Zawahiri to jihadist Internet forums June 25. In it, al Qaeda's deputy leader urges Muslims to support Palestinian militants by providing weapons and money, and by attacking U.S. and Israeli interests. Although al-Zawahiri's message is interesting, especially the fact that he urges support for an organization he has criticized heavily in the past, perhaps most telling about the release is that it contains no new video footage of al-Zawahiri himself.

In the 25-minute statement, al-Zawahiri discusses the importance of al-Quds (Jerusalem) to Muslims, and urges Muslims to unite with the "mujahideen in Palestine" (Hamas, Palestinian Islamic Jihad, etc.). Al-Zawahiri also calls on Hamas to establish a government based on Islamic law in Gaza, noting that, "Taking over power is not a goal, but a means to implement God's word on earth." The release begins with a snippet of an October 2001 video of al-Zawahiri and Osama bin Laden, but the bulk of the release consists of a still photograph of al-Zawahiri placed over a thin banner containing a small photo of the al-Aqsa Mosque.

The fact that al-Zawahiri chose this format rather than the more engaging and visually powerful video format suggests al Qaeda's apex leaders are feeling the heat of the campaign to locate and eliminate them. Although many people believe the al Qaeda leadership operates as it pleases along the Pakistani-Afghan border, evidence suggests otherwise.

Quantifying the Campaign

A June 20 report titled "The Quiet Campaign Against al Qaeda's Local Nodes" (see page 19) discussed the campaign conducted by the United States and its allies against al Qaeda's regional and local nodes. Though these efforts have been under way in many parts of the globe, the United States and its partners have been pursuing a concurrent campaign against al Qaeda's apex leadership, al Qaeda prime. Like the campaign against the regional nodes, the effort against the prime node employs all of the five prongs of the U.S. counterterrorism arsenal: military power, intelligence, economic sanctions, law enforcement operations and diplomacy.

The overall success of this campaign against al Qaeda prime has been hard to measure because there are few ways to take al Qaeda's pulse. By its nature, it is a secretive and nebulous organization that, in order to survive, has taken great pains to obscure its operations — especially since the invasion of Afghanistan in 2001 that flushed its leaders from their comfortable and well-appointed refuge inside the Taliban's Islamic republic.

While bin Laden and al-Zawahiri have escaped U.S.-led efforts to locate them, a large number of second-tier leaders and operatives have been captured or killed. This means the group's organizational chart has been altered dramatically below the top rung, making it difficult to determine the quality of the individuals who have been tapped to fill in the gaps. Publicly, al Qaeda has appointed American-born Adam Gadahn (known in jihadist circles as Azzam the American) as a principal spokesman. If the prime node has been forced to promote others of his caliber to operational leadership positions, the group could be in big trouble. However, with so many unknown players filling critical positions, it is difficult to determine precisely how much the attrition has affected the prime node's ability to plan and execute attacks.

Anecdotal evidence, however, suggests that their operational ability has been diminished. The group has not launched an attack using an al Qaeda "all-star team" since 9/11. Meanwhile, outside of Iraq and Afghanistan, the attacks conducted by its regional nodes, or by regional nodes working with operational commanders sent from al Qaeda prime, have decreased in frequency and impact over the past several months. The first six months of 2007 have been quieter than the first six months of 2006 and far more peaceful that the last six months of 2005. And, not to downplay the loss of life in London, Madrid, Bali and other places, but in terms of numbers, the death

AL QAEDA MESSAGES RELEASED VIA AS-SAHAB

	BIN LADEN/ AL ZAWAHIRI MESSAGES	VIDEO	AUDIO	TOTAL AS-SAHAB MESSAGES DURING THE TIME PERIOD
Pre-Damadola (18 mos) Sept. 2004-Jan. 2006	18	12	6	26
Post-Damadola (18 mos) Jan. 2006-June 2007	25	18	7	49
Pre-Damadola II (8 mos) Feb. 2006-Oct. 2006	15	14 (2 video intros included in 14)	1	27
Post-Damadola II (8 mos) Nov. 2006-June 2007	9	3	6	21

tolls and financial impacts of all those attacks do not hold a candle to the 9/11 attacks — even when many of them are combined.

Beyond the personnel losses al Qaeda has suffered, the loss of its dedicated training facilities in Afghanistan also has changed the way the prime node works. It is less autonomous and far more dependent on the largesse of Pakistani and Afghan feudal lords who control training camps along the border — and who are key to the security of al Qaeda prime. However, it is still difficult to pinpoint the impact this has had on al Qaeda's ability to operate.

Occasional glimpses into the organization made possible by intelligence efforts have provided some information on al Qaeda's health. For example, the seized July 2005 letter from al-Zawahiri to then-al Qaeda in Iraq leader Abu Musab al-Zarqawi, in which al-Zawahiri asks for financial assistance, demonstrates that al Qaeda's prime node was hurting for cash at the time. This state of affairs, a key objective of U.S. economic sanctions, likely was exacerbated by the Saudi government's action against al Qaeda supporters inside the kingdom, action prompted by attacks by al Qaeda's Saudi node.

Another way to gauge the health of the organization, or at least the comfort level of the group's apex leadership, is by looking at its public relations efforts and the statements it releases to the public. Al Qaeda prime has produced a steady supply of messages in order to keep local nodes — and perhaps more important, grassroots jihadists around the world — motivated. These releases, however, reveal a change over the last several months in the way al Qaeda communicates to the world.

As the chart (see page 28) illustrates, the number of messages from al Qaeda's two top leaders has fallen, while the use of video has dropped dramatically. Before the October 2006 missile attack in Chingai, Pakistan, 14 out of 15 messages were released in video format; since then, only three of the nine have included video. The switch to an audio format indicates concern about operational security. It also is noteworthy that bin Laden has not been heard from in any format, audio or video, since July 1, 2006 — nearly a year now. All these factors considered, it is apparent that the apex leadership feels threatened.

The Campaign on the Border

Al Qaeda leaders hiding along the Afghan-Pakistani border have good reason to be cautious. On June 19, an explosion killed at least 32 militants in Pakistan's mountainous Datta Khel district. Pakistani intelligence officials said 10 to 15 Arab and Turkmen militants were among the dead. According to sources, Abu Laith al-Libi, al Qaeda field commander in Afghanistan, was the target. DNA tests reportedly are being performed on the victims' remains in an effort to determine whether al-Libi is among them. If in fact he was killed in the strike, history suggests al Qaeda will release a statement confirming the death between June 29 and July 6.

The Datta Khel strike highlights the gravity of the threat faced by al Qaeda leaders hiding out in the area along the border. Other notable strikes include:

- Jan. 16, 2007: Pakistani army aviation units launch a predawn airstrike against a suspected militant camp near Zamzola in Pakistan's South Waziristan, killing 25 to 30 militants, including eight to 10 foreigners.

- Oct. 30, 2006: A missile strike against an Islamic school in Chingai, Pakistan, near the Afghan border, levels the building and kills at least 80 people. Sources say al-Zawahiri was the target.

- Jan. 13, 2006: A hellfire missile hits a home in Damadola, Pakistan, killing 18 people, including four senior al Qaeda operatives. The attack's intended target, al-Zawahiri, is not present.

- Dec. 4, 2005: Pakistani authorities say Hamza Rabia, reportedly al Qaeda's director of operations, is killed when a hellfire missile fired from a predator drone strikes a house in Haisori, North Waziristan.

- May 7, 2005: Haitham al-Yemeni, an al Qaeda operative who reportedly replaced Abu Farj al-Libi in al Qaeda's hierarchy after al-Libi's May 2, 2005, capture, is killed in a hellfire missile attack in North Waziristan.

• While not in the same region, al Qaeda's then-military chief Mohammed Atef also was killed in a hellfire missile strike by a CIA predator drone in eastern Afghanistan in November 2001.

Predator drones cannot be seen or heard by those on the ground. This means that a target's first indication that he is being attacked is the arrival of one or more supersonic, highly accurate and very destructive hellfire missiles. To those being targeted, the psychological impact of a weapon that can kill without warning is intense.

The Safe Bet

Shortly after the Chingai strike we noted a difference between al-Zawahiri's reaction to that strike and the Damadola strike. At the time, we said the Chingai strike hit very close to home, sent shockwaves through al Qaeda's operational security system and likely forced al-Zawahiri to go deeper underground. The numbers above appear to confirm that analysis.

We also speculated that the Damadola and Chingai strikes damaged As-Sahab's capabilities. One of those killed in the Damadola strike, Abdul al-Maghribi, was not only al-Zawahiri's son-in-law but also a senior As-Sahab manager. Despite these strikes, however, As-Sahab has released at least 13 video statements by al Qaeda leaders since the Chingai attack. Only three of these videos featured al-Zawahiri; the other 10 featured al Qaeda spokesmen such as Abu Yahya al-Libi, Azzam the American and the now possibly deceased Abu Laith al-Libi. As-Sahab also has released several other videos showing operations under way against U.S. forces in Afghanistan.

Regardless of these videos from Afghanistan, things have not been going well for the Taliban and their al Qaeda allies recently. Their much-touted spring offensive has largely fizzled and they have suffered many casualties on the battlefield against NATO forces in the south (the Canadians appear to have completed their learning

31

curve). The loss of charismatic, experienced battlefield commander Mullah Dadullah also will have an impact. Meanwhile, the Taliban have broken from traditional insurgent tactics with such things as suicide bombings, roadside bombings and attacks with vehicle-borne improvised explosive devices. This deviation suggests desperation on their part — which also would increase al Qaeda's angst.

Given that As-Sahab continues to release several videos each month, the lack of appearances by al-Zawahiri, and even bin Laden, is not the result of some scarcity of camera gear or video technicians. Indeed, there must be some other compelling reason for them to change their behavior — and fear that the forces hunting them are drawing close is a safe bet.

The U.S. National Intelligence Estimate of Al Qaeda
July 18, 2007

According to the National Intelligence Estimate (NIE) released July 17, the U.S. intelligence community believes that al Qaeda is still looking to attack targets that would have a significant economic, political and psychological impact on the United States. Furthermore, the report indicates that the U.S. intelligence community believes al Qaeda is capable of devising innovative ways to strike these targets.

The report reflects al Qaeda prime's targeting criteria. Rather than choosing targets based on military utility, al Qaeda generally chooses targets for their potential symbolic value in order to elicit the greatest political or psychological impact, which then translates into economic impact. For example, the U.S. State Department estimated that over the course of one year, the Sept. 11 attacks caused $120 billion in damage. That is the kind of economic damage al Qaeda wants to repeat. The Sept. 11 operation is estimated to have cost al Qaeda between $400,000 and $500,000.

Attacks in which large numbers of people are killed and maimed create the greatest psychological impact, as they generate graphic, provocative images that can be splashed across television screens and the front pages of newspapers. The Sept. 11 attack against the World Trade Center fit al Qaeda's psychological and economic criteria. The attack against Madrid's commuter rail system in 2004 met al Qaeda's political criterion in that it influenced Spain's decision to withdraw its military contingent from Iraq.

Bridges and other infrastructure targets could meet both symbolic and economic targeting criteria. After such an attack, a massive effort would be undertaken to repair the physical damage, but the lingering economic, political and social impact would be significant. The New York Stock Exchange, U.N. Headquarters and Citigroup Center building in New York City would fit the criteria for economic, mass-casualty and symbolic targets, as would the Chicago Mercantile Exchange, Chicago Board of Trade and Sears Tower. The International Monetary Fund and World Bank buildings in Washington, D.C., the U.S. Bank Tower (formerly known as the Library Tower) in California and Los Angeles International Airport also would make the list. Al Qaeda has already looked at these kinds of targets.

Softer targets such as hotels, theaters and places where large numbers of people gather could be attractive for mass-casualty attacks. However, the threat to these targets would more likely come from a grassroots amateur militant cell than from a cell sent by al Qaeda's apex leadership (although al Qaeda has surveilled the Waldorf-Astoria Hotel in New York City before, probably because of its higher-profile clientele, including diplomats and heads of state). Grassroots jihadists, such as the Fort Dix Six, focus on smaller, simpler and easier attacks. Theoretically, because of their relative simplicity, these plots are harder to detect. However, because they usually involve unskilled operatives who make amateur mistakes, such plots are often discovered during the planning stages of the attack cycle.

In the post-Sept. 11 world, with increased vigilance and intelligence collection focusing on potential jihadist threats, an elaborate attack involving multiple operatives originating overseas has a higher chance of being detected than before. So, while the large-scale strategic attacks that originate with al Qaeda prime are likely to be carried out by skilled operatives with a decent chance of success if they can evade detection, those attack plots are easier to discover.

The NIE also states that the U.S. intelligence community believes al Qaeda is "innovative in creating new capabilities and overcoming security obstacles" and that al Qaeda has been able to reconstitute its capabilities in the Afghanistan-Pakistan border area since 2001. This does not mean the organization is making use of specialized operatives trained to conduct covert operations inside the United States without being detected. Furthermore, the U.S. government continues to assume that al Qaeda's major concern is its effect on the United States. It still does not understand al Qaeda.

Obstacles to the Capture of Osama bin Laden
Sept. 12, 2007

Al Qaeda's As-Sahab media arm released a video Sept. 11 to commemorate the sixth anniversary of the 9/11 attacks. Although the 47-minute video features a voice-over introduction by Osama bin Laden, the bulk of it is of Abu Musab Waleed al-Shehri, one of the suicide bombers who crashed American Airlines Flight 11 into the World Trade Center's north tower. That recording was made prior to al-Shehri's travel to the United States in the spring of 2001.

There is nothing in bin Laden's audio segment to indicate it was recorded recently. The production does include a still photograph of him — one taken from what appears to be a real bin Laden video released Sept. 7 (in which he sports a dyed beard), but bin Laden's comments about the death of Abu Musab al-Zarqawi suggest they were recorded during al Qaeda's 2006 media blitz.

The release of two successive bin Laden messages, however, has again focused attention on bin Laden, who before last week had not been seen on video since late October 2004. This increased attention has once again caused people to question why the United States has failed to find bin Laden — and to wonder whether it ever will.

While the feds generally get their man in the movies or on television, it is very difficult in real life to find a single person who does not want to be found. It is even harder when that person is hiding in an extremely rugged, isolated and lawless area and is sheltered by a heavily armed local population.

The United States and Pakistan have not launched a major military operation to envelop and systematically search the entire region where bin Laden likely is hiding — an operation that would require tens of thousands of troops and likely result in heavy combat with the tribes residing in the area. Moreover, this is not the kind of operation they will take on in the future. The United States, therefore, will continue to pursue intelligence and conduct covert Special Forces operations, but if it is going to catch bin Laden, it will have to wait patiently for one of those operations to produce a lucky break — or for bin Laden to make a fatal operational security blunder.

Needle in a Haystack

Finding a single man in a large area with rugged terrain is a daunting task, even when a large number of searchers and a vast array of the latest high-tech surveillance equipment are involved. This principle was demonstrated by the manhunt for so-called "Olympic Bomber" Eric Rudolph, who was able to avoid one of the largest manhunts in U.S. history by hiding in North Carolina's Great Smoky Mountains. The task force looking for Rudolph at times had hundreds of federal, state and local law enforcement officers assigned to it, while some of its search operations involved thousands of law enforcement and volunteer searchers. The government also employed high-tech surveillance and sensor equipment and even offered a $1 million reward for information leading to Rudolph's capture.

However, Rudolph's capture in May 2003, more than five years after he was listed on the FBI's most-wanted list, was not the result of the organized search for him. Rather, he was caught by a rookie police officer on a routine patrol who found Rudolph rummaging for food in a dumpster behind a grocery store. The officer did not even realize he had captured Rudolph until he had taken him to the police station for booking.

Hostile Terrain

The terrain in the Smoky Mountains is tough and remote, but it is nothing compared to the terrain in the soaring, craggy Safed Koh range that runs along the Afghan-Pakistani border or in the Hindu Kush to the north. Some of the peaks in the Safed Koh range, including Mount Sikaram, are well over twice as high as any peak in the Smokies, while the Hindu Kush contains some of the highest peaks in the world.

But it is not only the terrain that is hostile. In the Great Smokies, there are some people who are not happy to see "revenuers" and other government agents — or other strangers, for that matter — but at least the area is under the federal government's control. The same cannot be said of the lawless areas along the Afghan-Pakistani border — the Federally Administered Tribal Areas (FATA) and North-West Frontier Province (NWFP). The presence of Pakistani military forces is resented in these areas, and troops are regularly attacked by the heavily armed tribesmen living there.

This is not a new phenomenon by any means. The Pashtun tribes in the rugged area along the Durand Line (drawn to demarcate the border between the British Raj and Afghanistan and that later became the Afghan-Pakistani border) have always been difficult to control. Even before the establishment of Pakistan, the inhabitants of the area gave the British colonial authorities fits for more than a century. The Britons were never able to gain full control over the region, so they granted extensive power to tribal elders, called maliks. Under the deal, the maliks retained their autonomy in exchange for maintaining peace between the tribesmen and the British Raj — thus allowing commerce to continue unabated.

However, some dramatic flare-ups of violence occurred against the Britons during their time in the region. One of the last of these flare-ups began in 1936 when a religious leader known as the Faqir of Ipi encouraged his followers to wage jihad on British forces. (Jihad against invading forces is a centuries-old tradition in the region.) The Faqir and his followers fought an extended insurgency against the British forces that ended only when they left Pakistan. The United Kingdom attempted to crush the Faqir and his followers, but the outmanned and outgunned insurgents used the rugged terrain and the support of the local tribes to their advantage. Efforts to use spies to locate or assassinate the Faqir also failed. Although the British and colonial troops pursuing the Faqir reportedly numbered more than 40,000 at one point, the Faqir was never captured or killed. He died a natural death in 1960.

A Modern Faqir?

Under U.S. pressure, the Pakistani military entered the FATA in force in March 2004 to pursue foreign militants — for the first time since the country's creation — but the operation resulted in heavy casualties for the Pakistani army, demonstrating how difficult it is for the Pakistani military to fight people so well integrated in the Pashtun tribal badlands. Following that failed operation, the Pakistani government reverted to the British model of negotiating with the maliks in an effort to combat the influence of the Taliban and foreign jihadists — and it has been harshly criticized because of it. Nowadays, jihadist insurgents are attacking Pakistani security and intelligence forces in the Pashtun areas in the Northwest.

The parallels between the hunt for the Faqir of Ipi and bin Laden are obvious — though it must be noted that bin Laden is a Saudi and not a native-born Pashtun. However, many of the challenges that the United Kingdom faced in that operation are also being faced by the United States today.

Aside from the terrain — a formidable obstacle in and of itself — U.S. forces are hampered by the strong, conservative Islamic conviction of the people in the region. This conviction extends beyond the tribes to include some members of the Pakistani military and Pakistan's intelligence agencies — especially those at the operational level in the region. It must be remembered that prior to 9/11 the Pakistani Inter-Services Intelligence agency and military openly supported the Taliban and their al Qaeda allies. In addition to the relationships formed between bin Laden and the so-called "Afghan Arabs" (foreign jihadists) during the war against the Soviets, Pakistani troops also trained and fought alongside the Taliban and al Qaeda in their battles against the Northern Alliance and other foes. Because of these deep and historic ties, there are some in the Pakistani government (specifically within the security apparatus) who remain sympathetic, if not outright loyal, to their friends in the Taliban and al Qaeda.

Additionally, and perhaps just as important, many in the Pakistani government and military do not want to kill their own people — the Pashtuns, for example — in order to destroy the much smaller subset of Pakistani and foreign militants. The challenge is to eliminate the militants while causing very little collateral damage to the rest of the population — and some in the Pakistani government say the airstrikes in places such as Chingai and Damadola have not accomplished this goal. In August, Pakistani Foreign Minister Khurshid Kasuri told television channel AAJ that Pakistan had done all it can in the war on terrorism and that, "No one should expect anything more from Islamabad."

In an operation such as the manhunt for bin Laden, intelligence is critical. However, the Taliban and al Qaeda so far have used their home-field advantage to establish better intelligence networks in the area than the Americans have. According to U.S. counterterrorism sources, U.S. intelligence gathered some very good leads in the early days of the hunt for bin Laden and other high-value al Qaeda targets, and they shared this intelligence with their counterparts in the Pakistani security apparatus to try to organize operations to act on the intelligence. During this process, people within the intelligence apparatus passed information back to al Qaeda, thus compromising the sources and methods being used to collect the information. These double agents inside the Pakistani government did grave damage to the U.S. human intelligence network.

Double agents within the Pakistani government are not the only problem, however. Following 9/11, there was a rapid increase in the number of case officers assigned to collect information pertaining to al Qaeda and bin Laden, and the CIA was assigned to be the lead agency in the hunt. One big problem with this, according to sources, was that most of these case officers were young, inexperienced and ill suited to the mission. The CIA really needed people who were more like Rudyard Kipling's character Kim — savvy case officers who understand the region's culture, issues and actors, and who can move imperceptibly within the local milieu to recruit valuable intelligence sources. Unfortunately for the CIA, it has been unable to find a real-life Kim.

This lack of seasoned, savvy and gritty case officers is complicated by the fact that, operationally, al Qaeda practices better security than do the Americans. First, there are few people permitted to see bin Laden and the other senior leaders, and most of those who are granted access are known and trusted friends and relatives. Someone else who wants to see bin Laden or another senior al Qaeda leader must wait while a message is first passed via a number of couriers to the organization. If a meeting is granted, the person is picked up at a time of al Qaeda's choosing and taken blindfolded via a circuitous route to a location where he is stripped and searched for bugs, beacons and other tracking devices. The person then reportedly is polygraphed to verify that his story is true. Only then will he be taken — blindfolded and via a circuitous route — to another site for the meeting. These types of measures make it very difficult for U.S. intelligence officers to get any of their sources close to the al Qaeda leaders, much less determine where they are hiding.

The areas where bin Laden likely is hiding are remote and insular. Visitors to the area are quickly recognized and identified — especially if they happen to be blond guys named Skip. Moreover, residents who spend too much time talking to such outsiders often are labeled as spies and killed. These conditions have served to ensure that the jihadists maintain a superior human intelligence (and counterintelligence) network in the area. It is a network that also stretches deep into the heart of Islamabad and Rawalpindi, Islamabad's twin city and home to the Pakistani army's general headquarters.

The Price of Security

Although al Qaeda's operational security and the jihadist intelligence network have been able to keep bin Laden alive thus far, they have lost a number of other senior operatives, including Khalid Sheikh Mohammed, Mohammed Atef, Abu Zubaydah, Ramzi bin al-Shibh, Abu Faraj al-Libi and others. Most of these have been al Qaeda operational managers, people who, by the very nature of their jobs, need to establish and maintain communications with militant cells.

This drive to recruit new jihadists to the cause and to help continue operational activity is what led to the lucky break that resulted in the 1995 arrest of Abdel Basit, the operational planner and bomb maker responsible for the 1993 World Trade Center bombing. Basit had tried to recruit a foreign student to assist him in one of the attempts to conduct "Operation Bojinka," a plan to bomb multiple U.S. airliners. Having gotten cold feet, the student revealed the plot, thus allowing Diplomatic Security special agents the opportunity to coordinate an operation to arrest Basit.

Al Qaeda has learned from the mistakes made by the men it has lost and has better secured the methods it uses to communicate with the outside world. This increased security, however, has resulted in increased insulation, which has adversely affected not only communications but also financial transfers and recruiting. Combined with U.S. efforts against al Qaeda, this has resulted in a reduction in operational ability and effectiveness.

The tension between operations and security poses a significant problem for an organization that seeks to maintain and manage a global militant network. By opting to err on the side of security, bin Laden and the others could escape capture indefinitely, though they would remain operationally ineffective. However, should they attempt to become more operationally active and effective — and decrease their security measures to do so — they will provide the United States with more opportunities to get the one break it needs to find bin Laden.

Al Qaeda, Afghanistan and the Good War
Feb. 25, 2008

There has been tremendous controversy over the U.S. invasion of Iraq, which consistently has been contrasted with Afghanistan. Many of those who opposed the Iraq war have supported the war in Afghanistan; indeed, they have argued that among the problems with Iraq is that it diverts resources from Afghanistan. Afghanistan has been seen as an obvious haven for terrorism. This has meant the war in Afghanistan often has been perceived as having a direct effect on al Qaeda and on the ability of radical Islamists to threaten the United States, while Iraq has been seen as unrelated to the main war. Supporters of the war in Iraq support the war in Afghanistan. Opponents of the war in Iraq also support Afghanistan. If there is a good war in our time, Afghanistan is it.

It is also a war that is in trouble. In the eyes of many, one of the Afghan war's virtues has been that NATO has participated as an entity. But NATO has come under heavy criticism from U.S. Defense Secretary Robert Gates for its performance. Some, like the Canadians, are threatening to withdraw their troops if other alliance members do not contribute more heavily to the mission. More important, the Taliban have been fighting an effective and intensive insurgency. Further complicating the situation, the roots of many of the military and political issues in Afghanistan are found across the border in Pakistan.

If the endgame in Iraq is murky, the endgame in Afghanistan is invisible. The United States, its allies and the Kabul government are fighting a holding action strategically. They do not have the force to destroy the Taliban — and in counterinsurgency, the longer the insurgents maintain their operational capability, the more likely they are to win. Further stiffening the Taliban resolve is the fact that, while insurgents have nowhere to go, foreigners can always decide to go home.

To understand the status of the war in Afghanistan, we must begin with what happened between 9/11 and early 2002. Al Qaeda had its primary command and training facilities in Afghanistan. The Taliban had come to power in a civil war among Afghans that broke out after the Soviet withdrawal. The Taliban had close links to the Pakistani Inter-Services Intelligence (ISI). While there was an ideological affinity between the two, there was also a geopolitical attraction. The Soviet invasion of Afghanistan concerned Pakistan gravely. India and the Soviets were aligned, and the Pakistanis feared being caught in a vise. The Pakistanis thus were eager to cooperate with the Americans and Saudis in supporting Islamist fighters against the Soviets. After the Soviets left and the United States lost interest in Afghanistan, the Pakistanis wanted to fill the vacuum. Their support of the Taliban served Pakistani national security interests and the religious proclivities of a large segment of the ISI.

After 9/11, the United States saw Afghanistan as its main problem. Al Qaeda, which was not Afghan but an international Islamist group, had received sanctuary from the Taliban. If the United States was to have any chance of defeating al Qaeda, it would be in Afghanistan. A means toward that end was destroying the Taliban government. This was not because the Taliban itself represented a direct threat to the United States but because al Qaeda's presence in Afghanistan did.

The United States wanted to act quickly and decisively in order to disrupt al Qaeda. A direct invasion of Afghanistan was therefore not an option. First, it would take many months to deploy U.S. forces. Second, there was no practical place to deploy them. The Iranians wouldn't accept U.S. forces on their soil and the Pakistanis were far from eager to see the Taliban toppled. Basing troops in Tajikistan, Uzbekistan and Turkmenistan along the northern border of Afghanistan was an option but also a logistical nightmare. It would be well into the spring of 2002 before any invasion was possible, and the fear of al Qaeda's actions in the meantime was intense.

The United States therefore decided not to invade Afghanistan. Instead, it made deals with groups that opposed the Taliban. In the North, Washington allied with the Northern Alliance, a group with close ties to the Russians. In the West, the United States allied with Persian groups under the influence of Iran. The United States made political arrangements with Moscow and Tehran to allow access to their Afghan allies. The Russians and Iranians both disliked the Taliban and were quite content to help. The mobilized Afghan groups also opposed the Taliban and loved the large sums of money U.S. intelligence operatives provided them.

These groups provided the force for the mission. The primary U.S. presence consisted of several hundred troops from U.S. Special Operations Command, along with CIA personnel. The United States also brought a great deal of air power, both Navy and Air Force, into the battle. The small U.S. ground force was to serve as a political liaison with the Afghan groups attacking the Taliban, to provide access to what weapons were available for the Afghan forces and, above all, to coordinate air support for the Afghans against concentrations of Taliban fighters. Airstrikes began a month after 9/11.

While Washington turned out an extraordinary political and covert performance, the United States did not invade. Rather, it acquired armies in Afghanistan prepared to carry out the mission and provided them with support and air power. The operation did not defeat the Taliban. Instead, it forced them to make a political and military decision.

Political power in Afghanistan does not come from the cities. It comes from the countryside, while the cities are the prize. The Taliban could defend the cities only by massing forces to block attacks by other Afghan factions. But when they massed their forces, the Taliban were vulnerable to air attacks. After experiencing the consequences of

U.S. air power, the Taliban made a strategic decision. In the absence of U.S. airstrikes, they could defeat their adversaries and had done so before. While they might have made a fight of it, given U.S. air power, the Taliban selected a different long-term strategy.

Rather than attempt to defend the cities, the Taliban withdrew, dispersed and made plans to regroup. Their goal was to hold enough of the countryside to maintain their political influence. As in their campaign against the Soviets, the Taliban understood that their Afghan enemies would not pursue them, and that over time, their ability to conduct small-scale operations would negate the value of U.S. airpower and draw the Americans into a difficult fight on unfavorable terms.

The United States was not particularly disturbed by the outcome. It was not after the Taliban but al Qaeda. It appears — and much of this remains murky — that the command cell of al Qaeda escaped from Afghan forces and U.S. Special Operations personnel at Tora Bora and slipped across the border into Pakistan. Exactly what happened is unclear, but it is clear that al Qaeda's command cell was not destroyed. The fight against al Qaeda produced a partial victory. Al Qaeda clearly was disrupted and relocated — and was denied its sanctuary. A number of its operatives were captured, further degrading its operational capability.

The Afghan campaign therefore had these outcomes:

- Al Qaeda was degraded but not eliminated.
- The Taliban remained an intact fighting force, but the United States never really expected them to commit suicide by massing for U.S. B-52 strikes.
- The United States had never invaded Afghanistan and had made no plans to occupy it.
- Afghanistan was never the issue, and the Taliban were a subordinate matter.

• After much of al Qaeda's base lost its sanctuary in Afghanistan and had to relocate to Pakistan, the war in Afghanistan became a sideshow for the U.S. military.

Over time, the United States and NATO brought about 50,000 troops to Afghanistan. Their hope was that Hamid Karzai's government would build a force that could defeat the Taliban. But the problem was that, absent U.S. and NATO forces, the Taliban had managed to defeat the forces now arrayed against them once before, in the Afghan civil war. The U.S. commitment of troops was enough to hold the major cities and conduct offensive operations that kept the Taliban off balance, but the United States could not possibly defeat them. The Soviets had deployed 300,000 troops in Afghanistan and could not defeat the mujahideen. NATO, with 50,000 troops and facing the same shifting alliance of factions and tribes that the Soviets couldn't pull together, could not pacify Afghanistan.

But vanquishing the Taliban simply was not the goal. The goal was to maintain a presence that could conduct covert operations in Pakistan looking for al Qaeda and keep al Qaeda from returning to Afghanistan. Part of this goal could be achieved by keeping a pro-American government in Kabul under Karzai. The strategy was to keep al Qaeda off balance, preserve Karzai and launch operations against the Taliban designed to prevent them from becoming too effective and aggressive. The entire U.S. military would have been insufficient to defeat the Taliban; the war in Afghanistan thus was simply a holding action.

This holding action was made all the more difficult by the fact that the Taliban could not be isolated from their sources of supply or sanctuary; Pakistan provided both. It really didn't matter whether this was because President Pervez Musharraf's government intended to play both sides, whether factions inside the Pakistani military maintained close affinities with the Taliban or whether the Pakistani government and army simply couldn't control tribal elements loyal to al Qaeda. What did matter was that all along the Afghan border — particularly

45

in southern Afghanistan — supplies flowed in from Pakistan, and the Taliban moved into sanctuaries in Pakistan for rest and regrouping.

The Taliban were and are operating on their own terrain. They have excellent intelligence about the movements of NATO forces and a flexible and sufficient supply line allowing them to maintain and increase operations and control of the countryside. Having retreated in 2001, the Taliban systematically regrouped, rearmed and began operating as a traditional guerrilla force with an increased penchant for suicide attacks.

As in Vietnam, the challenge in fighting a guerrilla force is to cut it off from its supplies. The United States failed to interdict the Ho Chi Minh Trail, and that allowed men and materiel to move into South Vietnam until the United States lost the appetite for war. In Afghanistan, it is the same problem compounded. First, the lines of supply into Pakistan are even more complex than the Ho Chi Minh trail was. Second, the country that provides the supplies is formally allied with the United States. Pakistan is committed both to cutting those lines of supply and aiding the United States in capturing al Qaeda in its Northwest. That is the primary mission, but the subsidiary mission remains keeping the Taliban within tolerable levels of activity and preventing them from posing a threat to more and more of the Afghan countryside and cities. There has been a great deal of focus on Pakistan's assistance in its own northwestern regions against al Qaeda, but much less on the lines of supply maintaining the Taliban in southern Afghanistan. And as Pakistan has attempted to pursue a policy of balancing its relations with the Taliban and with the United States, the Pakistani government now faces a major jihadist insurgency on its own turf.

Afghanistan therefore is not — and in some ways never has been — the center of gravity of the challenge facing the United States. Occupying Afghanistan is inconceivable without a fundamental shift in Pakistan's policies or capabilities. But forcing Pakistan to change its policies in southern Afghanistan really is pointless, since the United States doesn't have enough forces there to take advantage of a Pakistani shift, and Washington doesn't care about the Taliban in the long run.

The real issue is the hardest to determine. Is al Qaeda prime — not al Qaeda enthusiasts or sympathizers who are able to carry out local suicide bombings, but the capable covert operatives we saw on 9/11 — still operational? And even if it is degraded, given enough time, will al Qaeda be able to regroup and ramp up its operational capability? If so, then the United States must maintain its posture in Afghanistan, as limited and unbalanced as it is. The United States might even need to consider extending the war to Pakistan in an attempt to seal the border if the Taliban continue to strengthen. But if al Qaeda is not operational, then the rationale for guarding Kabul and Karzai becomes questionable.

We have no way of determining whether al Qaeda remains operational; we are not sure anyone can assess that with certainty. Certainly, we have not seen significant operations for a long time, and U.S. covert capabilities should have been able to weaken al Qaeda over the past seven years. But if al Qaeda remains active, capable and in northwestern Pakistan, then the U.S. presence in Afghanistan will continue.

As the situation in Iraq settles down — and it appears to be doing so — more focus will be drawn to Afghanistan, the war that even opponents of Iraq have acknowledged as appropriate and important. But it is important to understand what this war consists of: It is a holding action against an enemy that cannot be defeated (absent greater force than is available) with open lines of supply into a country allied with the United States. It is a holding action waiting for certain knowledge of the status of al Qaeda, knowledge that likely will not come. Afghanistan is a war without exit and a war without victory. The politics are impenetrable, and it is even difficult to figure out whether allies like Pakistan are intending to help or are capable of helping.

Thus, while it may be a better war than Iraq in some sense, it is not a war that can be won or even ended. It just goes on.

CHAPTER 2: CONNECTIONS

Al Qaeda's Western Recruits
June 24, 2004

Al Qaeda remains a dynamic organization that leverages local expertise and resources in surveilling, planning and carrying out operations. To that end, the group seeks indigenous operatives to carry out pre-strike surveillance and attacks in several nations. An examination of some of these Western recruits provides insights into al Qaeda's methods of recruiting, coordinating, planning and deploying resources.

There are many suspected American and other Western al Qaeda facilitators, operatives and sympathizers. High-profile cases that prove especially insightful include those of:

- Jose Padilla, an American known as the "Dirty Bomber."

- Richard Reid, a Briton known as the "Shoe Bomber."

- Jack Roche, Australia's "Reluctant Militant," who reportedly has ties to al Qaeda and Jemaah Islamiyah.

Drawing from statements given to investigators, each of these cases has similarities and differences — the most striking similarity being that the suspects were all caught. Though a look at these three offers some insights into al Qaeda's Western recruitment, it should not be assumed that this assessment covers all of the group's recruiting and training techniques. The very fact that these men were caught raises questions — and even suggests al Qaeda was fully cognizant of the potential for detection. The stories of those not yet caught could prove much more interesting and insightful.

Jose Padilla, the Dirty Bomber

Born in 1970 in New York, Padilla had a troubled childhood that led to gang involvement and run-ins with police in Chicago and Florida. In 1992 he was introduced to Islam — reportedly by his manager at a fast food restaurant in Florida — though some stories suggest that the introduction occurred while he was serving jail time. By 1993, Padilla had changed his name to Ibrahim and become involved with radical Islamists in the Ft. Lauderdale area.

In 1996, Padilla married and acquired a U.S. passport. Reports indicate that he and his wife lived in a gated community, despite neither having a job — suggesting that Padilla already was receiving some kind of stipend from the Islamic community. In 1998, he left his wife and traveled to Egypt. He stayed there for just more than a year, marrying an Egyptian woman before heading to Pakistan. Once again, he took a new name — Abdullah al-Muhajir (Abdullah the Immigrant).

While in Pakistan, Padilla met a Yemeni who introduced him to another al Qaeda recruiter. This acquaintance sponsored Padilla's trip to Afghanistan for weapons training at a camp overseen by Abu Zubaida. There, he was given on-the-job training as a Taliban guard near Kabul — apparently a test of his loyalty. Afterward, Padilla was approached by Mohammed Atef, who began determining the Westerner's commitment and possible use as an operative.

Padilla was chosen as a potential operative only after he had completed basic training in Afghanistan. This trend seems to follow that of most Western al Qaeda recruits. As will be seen with the case of Jack Roche, the direct recruitment of operatives in Western nations is difficult, and waiting for disaffected or otherwise exploitable Westerners to make their way to al Qaeda is preferable.

What came next for Padilla appears to be another common trend in al Qaeda recruiting. He was sent to Pakistan, where he reported a lost passport and was issued a new one without stamps that tracked his previous travels. Padilla then went on an expense-paid trip back to Egypt to visit his wife — an obvious perk and attempt on al Qaeda's part to continue the bond with the American al Qaeda recruit. Two months later, Padilla was back in Afghanistan to receive his first assignment: blowing up U.S. apartment buildings with a combination of natural gas leaks and detonators.

At this point, Padilla's potential as an operative began to slip. He had a falling out with his assigned partner, Jafar al-Tayer. (Padilla later said that Jafar was probably an American.) After training for the operation, the two argued. Padilla then told his handlers that the operation was off, since he could not carry it out alone. This training occurred just before the Sept. 11 attacks in the United States. It is unclear whether the attacks affected the men's decision to call off the gas explosion attacks.

Later in the year, as U.S. air strikes in Afghanistan began, Padilla fled to Pakistan. There, he and another militant attempted to sell the idea of detonating a nuclear bomb in America. The two told Abu Zubaida about instructions for building a nuclear device they had seen on the Internet. Abu Zubaida had doubts about this idea and assigned them to carry out the long-overdue apartment bombings instead. But by this time, it appears Padilla was no longer willing to listen.

The idea of detonating a nuclear weapon — or at least a radiological device — was presented to Khalid Sheikh Mohammed by Padilla in March 2002. Again, it was rejected in favor of the apartment attacks. After several rounds of discussion, al Qaeda gave Padilla and an associate each $20,000 and sent them on their way. Two months later, Padilla was arrested while entering the United States; Abu Zubaida — by then in custody — had informed investigators of his activities.

51

After turning down the more easily carried out apartment attacks, Padilla became useless as an al Qaeda operative. But as a red herring for U.S. security forces to spend resources and time on, he served a purpose. He also represented a worst-case scenario — a converted Muslim militant who did not fit the racial profiling designed to weed out possible al Qaeda operatives.

Richard Reid, the Shoe Bomber

The son of a Jamaican father and an English mother, Richard Reid was born and raised in a London suburb. Reid's father — reportedly also a convert to Islam — spent much of his time in jail. By the mid 1990s, Reid had also embarked on a life of crime and was incarcerated for a series of muggings. While serving time in the Feltham Young Offenders' Institute, he was introduced to, and embraced, Islam.

Like Padilla, Reid came from an essentially fatherless home, became a juvenile petty criminal and turned to Islam while serving time. Islam provided a sense of belonging and purpose for both men; however, their apparent lack of self-discipline also opened them up to the influence of radicals.

Reid — who changed his name to Abdel Rahim — joined the Brixton Mosque, which helped rehabilitate former criminals. His devotion to studying drew him to more radical members of the Islamic community. Reid began accusing mosque members and leaders of deviating from the truth and accepting Western influences. Before being expelled from the mosque, he met up with fellow disaffected worshiper Zacarias Moussaoui.

In late 1998, Reid stopped attending Brixton and moved to Pakistan. He then began training in Afghanistan and traveled to several countries — including Egypt, Israel, Turkey, Belgium, the Netherlands and France. During these flights, Reid was allegedly scouting the security procedures of American airlines; he also visited radical and militant Islamist communities. While in Afghanistan, Reid trained in a special camp for solo martyrs, learning bomb making and methods of avoiding detection. One of his supervisors was Khalid Sheikh Mohammed. Before departing from Paris in December 2001, Reid acquired a new passport free of stamps from his previous travels. Like Padilla, he claimed to have lost his original passport. Reid was detained briefly for questioning at the Paris airport Dec. 21 — the original date of his planned attack — but was allowed to fly the next day. He reportedly was unsuccessful in his attack only because the required fuses got wet in the rain.

Reid appeared to have better training than Padilla, who basically became a "blown agent" left on his own by al Qaeda. (If he had managed to pull off an attack, however, al Qaeda would not have complained.) Perhaps more important, Reid was more willing to die.

Despite these differences, Padilla and Reid followed a similar path to al Qaeda. Impressionable young men, they flirted with Islam in prison and gravitated toward those with the strongest convictions in their respective Islamic communities. Al Qaeda did not need to seek out these Western members. The group simply moved them in a natural progression through the training camps in Afghanistan to selection as operatives.

Jack Roche, Australia's Reluctant Militant

Jack Roche's case bears similarities and differences to those of Padilla and Reid. Born in 1953 as Paul George Holland, Roche was much older upon his introduction to Islam. A native of Britain, he drifted to Germany and eventually to Australia, where he obtained citizenship in 1978. Though he had few if any problems with the law, Roche was a heavy drinker. He converted to Islam in 1993 as part of an effort to tackle his drinking problem.

As was the case with Padilla and Reid, Roche turned to Islam to fill a void and get on a more "correct" path. All three men proved susceptible to external influences in their newfound religion and lifestyle.

From 1993 to 1995, Roche lived in Indonesia, studying Islam and teaching English as a second language. He met Abdullah Sungkar

— co-founder of Jemaah Islamiyah (JI) — while the latter was visiting a Sydney mosque in 1996. Roche then began to affiliate with the more radical Islamists and JI. In early 2000, he traveled to Afghanistan and joined the Taliban. Mohammad Atef and other senior al Qaeda members asked him to establish an al Qaeda cell in Australia, where he could stake out the Israeli Embassy and other potential targets.

The use and deployment of Roche then fell apart, apparently because of splits between and within JI and al Qaeda. Roche was sent to Malaysia in February 2000 to meet with Hambali, an operative for both al Qaeda and JI. Hambali told Roche to prepare for a trip to Afghanistan where he would meet a "sheikh." Roche returned to Australia, flew back to Malaysia a month later, and then went on to Pakistan, where he was met by Khalid Sheikh Mohammed. In April, Roche went to Afghanistan, where he met Osama bin Laden and undertook a two-week course in explosives.

Roche's relationship with JI seems to have accelerated al Qaeda's decision to take him in as a potential operative and cell leader. He discussed possible targets inside Australia with al Qaeda leaders, including Mohammed Atef and Khalid Sheikh Mohammed. Roche was given more than $8,000 and was told to begin surveillance on the Israeli Embassy and other key Israeli diplomatic and economic targets. However, reports indicate his JI handlers were actually more interested in the Sydney Olympics.

After embarking on the surveillance work in June 2000, Roche became apprehensive about carrying out an actual operation; he was also experiencing little luck in recruiting new cell members. On July 14, Roche phoned the Australian Security Intelligence Organization (ASIO). He explained his connection with bin Laden and warned that a JI and al Qaeda cell existed in Australia. Roche called again five days later, after receiving no response to his first call.

On Aug. 8, recognizing Roche's growing reluctance, JI urged him to carry on with the operation. Two days later, Roche again called the ASIO. Again, he received no response. A few days later, JI called off the attack plans. Roche was left on his own until his arrest more than two years later.

Though Roche's mission was eventually called off, neither JI nor al Qaeda did anything — aside from issuing minor threats — to ensure that he never talked. For an organization as security conscious as al Qaeda, this seems an anomaly. Perhaps the group wanted Roche to be caught as a means of spreading fear in Australia. On the other hand, al Qaeda might have had little concern over his capture; after all, ASIO failed to respond to his phone calls.

Common Denominators

The common denominators in these three cases are not socio-economic conditions or age. Rather, they are a perceived need for belonging to something, a vulnerability and naïveté that left the three men susceptible to radical teachings. Radical white hate groups and other cults also recruit members by tapping into these kinds of vulnerabilities.

Though many Westerners convert to Islam, only a small number of them are enticed by its radical teachings. A still smaller number actually act on these teachings, receiving training in places such as Pakistan, Afghanistan or Indonesia and transitioning from radicalism to militantism. Still fewer become al Qaeda operatives — a step that requires denouncing one's own nation in favor of a broader ideology.

Al Qaeda's Communications Network
Aug. 11, 2004

The arrests of several suspected al Qaeda members and supporters in Pakistan, the United Kingdom, the United Arab Emirates and the southern United States offer a snapshot of a sliver of al Qaeda's command, control and communications network.

Coupled with previous information gleaned from arrests, threats and successful attacks, it reveals an organization with both a highly controlling centralized core and a level of operational freedom for its regional and local commanders. Central to its effectiveness in turning deep strategic thinking at the core into tactical operations on the ground is a series of communications nodes — people prized not so much for their ability to plan but for their skill with computers.

The communications nodes are reservoirs of information collected from far-flung operatives via e-mail or hand-delivered messages. The information is processed, stored and disseminated to other operatives or to the core al Qaeda leadership. Messages are delivered from the al Qaeda core down the chain of command to the regional and local field commanders. While there often are several intermediary couriers, the communications nodes are the central link between a strategic vision and a tactical reality.

Pakistan's arrest of key communications node Mohammad Naeem Noor Khan on July 13 offered intelligence agencies a treasure-trove of insight into not only al Qaeda's potential plans and surveillance methods but also the structure of at least part of its network. Khan's computer carried al Qaeda surveillance reports and contact information for commanders — which Pakistani and U.S. intelligence agencies exploited by engaging Khan in an operation to flush out these disparate commanders.

Khan sent messages to locations around the world, saying he had new information from al Qaeda central and was waiting for replies. These probes into the system, monitored closely by Inter-Services Intelligence (ISI) and the CIA, led to the detentions of both Ahmed Khalfan Ghailani, a Tanzanian linked to the U.S. Embassy bombings in Africa, and Abu Eisa al-Hindi, a regional militant commander in the United Kingdom and probably the United States. Further probes likely revealed clues about the communications paths and perhaps pointed to other regional or local commanders. However, the revelation of Khan's arrest by U.S. politicians a day after the heightened terrorist alerts were issued for New York, New Jersey and Washington, D.C., quickly dried up the flow of information, frustrating the ISI, the Pakistani government and the CIA.

Khan provides an example of the kind of communications network al Qaeda has established — and, undoubtedly, several other Khans are out there. They do not necessarily know the names or whereabouts of the commanders, or of Osama bin Laden or other top al Qaeda officials, but they are aware of the plans and orders being passed back and forth.

Given al Qaeda's penchant for security and for redundancy of operations, there likely is overlap in the field commanders on the contact list of each of these communications nodes, which allows a steady flow of directions from the top and information and intelligence from the field even if one node is compromised. As a built-in security feature, al Qaeda field commanders and tactical operatives flee or go underground when their line of communication seems suspect or dries up. They do not strike with whatever plan they might have been plotting.

This reveals a certain level of central control and a lack of clarity by the tactical operatives about the exact nature of al Qaeda's plans; they train for a certain type of operation, they survey certain areas, but the exact timing, location and coordination of several cells is done by a regional or local field commander. This is done is such a way that even if one militant or cell were broken, it would not necessarily jeopardize the entire operation.

This security feature also means that each person in the communications and command chain might know the true identities of only a few other operatives. If one operative is interrogated, rather than giving up the whole network, he can provide only an e-mail address or the names of a few others — thus delaying the unraveling of a broader swath of the network. If these communications lines jump across continents while arrests take place, other links in that chain will be broken and new communications paths will be established.

Once a key arrest has been made public, or a series of arrests takes place, all other al Qaeda operatives with connections to that link in the network go underground, leaving investigators only a short time to round up a few others. That partly explains the sudden drop in detentions following the rapid roundup of operational cells in Pakistan and the United Kingdom.

The Pakistani cell broken by the information from Khan was nominally directed by Ahmed Khalfan Ghailani. Ghailani was one of the FBI's most-wanted al Qaeda operatives, accused of being a key planner and facilitator in the 1998 U.S. Embassy attacks in Kenya and Tanzania. His high profile, however, left him out of the al Qaeda inner circle for planning — though he remains one of the most loyal to bin Laden. Instead, after a stint raising funds in Africa, Ghailani had lain low, taking advantage of the broad Islamist support network to move about and avoid capture.

Ghailani apparently had two more recent roles in Pakistan. First, he was senior adviser to local al Qaeda militants and operational commanders in the campaign against Pakistani President Gen. Pervez Musharraf and his regime. He also was as a key recruiter for al Qaeda members from Africa.

Abu Eisa al-Hindi, however, is a much more active operational commander, similar in role to Mohammad Atta, who coordinated the final stages of the Sept. 11 attacks. Al-Hindi was most recently based in the United Kingdom but has traveled to the United States, and like Atta he probably had operational control over several cells on both sides of the Atlantic. Al-Hindi coordinated and participated in the surveillance of key U.S. buildings, traveling to the United States at least once in 2001. Once the information was collected, the final surveillance dossiers would have been transmitted, through Khan, back to the core al Qaeda leadership, where a strategic assessment of the possible tactical targets could be conducted. Further surveillance — or attack planning — was then transmitted back through Khan or another communications node to al-Hindi.

Although al-Hindi's Aug. 4 arrest also nabbed several suspected al Qaeda members in England, it thus far has failed to turn up any major operatives inside the United States. In fact, though he allegedly sent at least six messages to U.S.-based operatives or commanders during the flushing operation, none has led to U.S. arrests, though a few people might now be under surveillance. Once Khan's arrest became public knowledge, these operatives and commanders undoubtedly dropped off the radar screen, and intelligence officials have said the general background "chatter" of al Qaeda members fell precipitously with word of Khan's detention.

Given that al Qaeda operatives have entered the United States at least a year in advance of any potential attack, the fact that this particular communications link has been broken does not necessarily preclude an operation already in its final stages. Atta, for example, entered the United States on June 3, 2000, and exited and re-entered the country several times, meeting with other al Qaeda operatives all over the world. Officials know Khan was in contact with several people in the United States and around the world — but their identities and exact locations remain unknown.

Al Qaeda almost definitely has dozens of "sleeper agents" inside the United States — they probably have been in the country for years, waiting to be called up. Only when a cell leader moves into the country and begins contacting these sleepers will they learn of their mission and its details. It might never be known for sure whether al-Hindi's arrest has thwarted a major operation.

Ultimately, Khan's detention has offered useful insights into the internal workings of al Qaeda. First, there are innumerable layers of command, control and communication inside al Qaeda, obfuscating the true origin and end-point of messages and concealing the identities of operatives. There are lowest-level, grunt-work operatives, mid-level directors and senior planners. There also are fund-raisers, communications people and deliverymen who only carry messages.

Second, the sender almost never delivers Al Qaeda messages to the end recipient. A piece of paper written in code could travel from Lahore, Pakistan, to UAE to Britain to the United States, carried by a different person on each leg. Surveillance done by an operative at a Las Vegas casino might be e-mailed to an operative in Nigeria, who forwards it to an account based in Yemen, who forwards it to an account in Pakistan. Again, the purpose is to conceal and, in case of detection or penetration, secure the network.

But it also means al Qaeda is rather reliant on its key communications nodes for rapid and efficient dissemination of information and orders. The detection and disabling of these nodes, even without a subsequent operation to flush out their contacts, can cause a serious disruption of al Qaeda's capabilities. With the current operating paradigm being to go underground if a breach in the network is believed, the capture of communications people might be the most effective way of undermining al Qaeda's operational capabilities — shy of the capture of bin Laden himself.

Al Qaeda's Link to the London Bombers
Sept. 21, 2005

British police released surveillance footage Sept. 20 that they say shows Mohammad Sidique Khan, Shehzad Tanweer and Germaine Lindsay conducting a dry run in preparation for the July 7 London bombings. The tape, recorded June 28, shows the three men entering Luton station before traveling to King's Cross station — the same routes they took July 7.

Citing a lack of a direct forensic link between the bombers and known al Qaeda operatives, some in the intelligence and law enforcement community have suggested that the Underground bombers were not connected to al Qaeda and that, by claiming responsibility for the attack, deputy al Qaeda leader Ayman al-Zawahiri attempted to give the network undue credit. Although it is fairly certain that the four bombers had no direct connection to the higher-level al Qaeda leadership, the methods used in the attack suggest that it was an al Qaeda operation and sanctioned by the network's leadership.

The fact that a rehearsal did take place before the actual attack demonstrates that the operatives were not complete novices — as some also have suggested — but that they had some degree of training and organization. Moreover, staging a practice run is consistent with the kind of meticulous planning that has characterized large-scale al Qaeda operations. Similar dry runs and pre-operational surveillance were carried out before the August 1998 bombings of the

U.S. embassies in Kenya and Tanzania and the Sept. 11 attacks. The bombing of Philippine Airlines flight 434 in December 1994 also was a dry run for a more ambitious al Qaeda operation codenamed "Bojinka" — a plan to bomb multiple airplanes simultaneously over the Pacific Ocean.

Khan, the alleged leader of the July 7 bombers, made a videotape before the operation in which he explains his motivation for carrying out the attack. Khan possibly made his statement while in Pakistan, where he is alleged to have traveled in 2004 to meet with al Qaeda operatives. A second segment of the same tape contained an al-Zawahiri statement in which he praised the attack but stopped short of claiming credit — possibly because it had not yet happened. Al-Zawahiri's presence on the Khan tape, which Arab satellite television Al Jazeera aired Sept. 1, is another link between the July 7 attack and the al Qaeda leadership — although it should be noted that the two never appear together in the tape. In addition, al-Zawahiri has appeared in two other tapes in which he speaks of the London bombings. In the latest one, released Sept. 19, he clearly claims responsibility for the attacks on behalf of al Qaeda — something the jihadist network rarely does.

An al Qaeda operation as important as an attack against a Western capital certainly would have the foreknowledge and blessing of the network's highest leadership. Even though the leaders knew of and endorsed the operation, however, they would not necessarily have had direct contact with the operatives who carried out the attack. They likely received reports on the progress of the operation and issued orders to at least one mid-level operative or tactical commander, who in turn supervised and handled the attackers, including Khan. Although not involved with the tactical details of their attacks, al Qaeda leadership has always had a role in the operations. Khan, whose role in the organization would have been that of a foot soldier, would probably not have met al Zawahiri or al Qaeda leader Osama bin Laden.

Al Qaeda is similar to the Mafia, in that foot soldiers generally are not granted the privilege of meeting the godfather immediately after they are inducted into the family. This is especially true for al Qaeda, since the post-Sept. 11 environment has forced senior al Qaeda members to dramatically increase their operational security. In this case, in which the "godfather" is the world's most wanted man, the foot soldiers would not be allowed near him unless a dire operational need arose.

The surveillance images of the July 7 bombers' dry run provide further evidence of al Qaeda links with the deadly attack. The camera recordings also show that, despite difficulties in communicating and operating since the October 2001 U.S.-led invasion of its home base in Afghanistan, al Qaeda still retains enough command-and-control capability to stage the occasional large-scale attack against a Western city.

The Web of Jihad: Strategic Utility and Tactical Weakness
June 14, 2006

With the death last week of Abu Musab al-Zarqawi, the world has been focused on the future of his al Qaeda in Iraq organization. And while that is an important question, particularly as it relates to the security situation in Iraq, it is fitting also to reflect on the history and impact of al-Zarqawi's violent movement. The group has been, of course, well-known for conducting frequent suicide bombings in Iraq and the simultaneous suicide strikes at three hotels in Jordan last fall, but its brutality is not necessarily what made al-Zarqawi a household name. That came about largely because of al Qaeda in Iraq's skillful use of the Internet. It has embraced technology in a way heretofore unprecedented for any jihadist group.

In addition to posting shocking videos of decapitations to the Web, the "information wing" of al-Zarqawi's group routinely posted statements (often several in a single day), videos of suicide operations and ambushes and eulogies praising and glorifying suicide operatives. It even published a monthly Web magazine. The information wing of al Qaeda in Iraq has been able to put a slick, professional face on the cause of the larger al Qaeda organization — while also documenting achievements on the battlefield, inculcating readers with the theology of jihadism and enticing new recruits to join the jihadist struggle.

This use of technology has played into the evolution of the jihadist movement and may now be helping to foster new incarnations of al Qaeda. But just as significantly, use of the Internet has certain drawbacks. There is only so much that can be done in cyberspace. Tactical realities and operational security concerns mandate that some activities must be conducted in the physical world — and it is at this juncture, in making the transition from virtual to actual reality, that newer actors could well be at their most vulnerable.

The Internet and Jihadists

In his use of the Internet, al-Zarqawi stood out even from other top al Qaeda leaders like Osama bin Laden and Ayman al-Zawahiri, who still rely on more standard Arabic-language media outlets (notably Al Jazeera TV) to distribute important messages. The information wing of al-Zarqawi's group posted his statements directly to professional-looking Web sites of their own creation — and, proportionally, did so in far greater quantities than the core al Qaeda group. Granted, location and amenities were in all probability a key factor; al-Zarqawi's node in Iraq has been operating in an urban environment, while bin Laden and al-Zawahiri are believed to be hiding in the rugged hinterlands along the Afghan-Pakistani border. Nevertheless, the younger group's embrace of technology seems to transcend that geographical difference to reflect a philosophical and perhaps even generational difference.

Within this vein, al Qaeda in Iraq has used the Internet in two very significant ways: to disseminate propaganda in real time, and to shape public perceptions and debate in both the Islamic and Western spheres. In other words, the Web has been a timely, efficient and effective tool for conducting information warfare, which is key for breaking the will of the enemy and in motivating one's own forces.

That said, the use of the Web by jihadist groups far predates al Qaeda in Iraq. With the launch in 1996 of the Azzam.com Web site — so named in honor of bin Laden's mentor — jihadists had a professional-looking "store front" that allowed them to provide inspiration, news and instruction to adherents and potential recruits, and which became a channel for others to initiate contact with jihadist groups. Azzam.com became an important mechanism through which funds for jihadist groups could be raised and willing volunteers could find ways to link up with jihadist groups in places like Chechnya and Bosnia. It also provided tips on steps to take in order to attend militant training camps run by organizations like al Qaeda.

Following the 9/11 attacks, there was a virtual explosion of jihadist activity on the Web — ranging from chat rooms and blogs that became popular with "jihadist cheerleaders" to sites run by actual members of militant groups. Many of these jihadist "cyberwarriors" are in their late teens or early twenties, and many of them have been educated in the West. Some of the cyberwarriors — like Younis Tsouli, the British citizen using the handle "Irhabi007" — discover jihadism online and then move on to join the cause in the real world. Often, they join or form grassroots cells and become what we have labeled "al Qaeda Version 3.0 or 4.0" operatives.

As we have discussed, the Internet has been a great enabler for grassroots cells to spread their ideology and recruit new acolytes — and, indeed, it also seems to have given them the ability to network across oceans and borders. However, the Internet often has proved to be an Achilles' heel for clandestine groups as well. This is an area that warrants some study.

Risks and Limitations

From a tactical perspective, there are some things that simply cannot be done over the Internet — either for practical reasons or in light of operational security considerations.

For example, recruiting a new member into a cell can be a very risky activity under any circumstances — and even more dangerous in the "virtual world." At any point, a jihadist or organized crime group might find it has opened itself up to someone who can't keep a secret, whose loyalties are suspect or who can be bought for the right price. These risks go up considerably in cyberspace. People on the Internet are not always who they portray themselves to be (just ask anyone who's had a bad online dating experience). For the jihadist recruiter, then, it can be extremely difficult to determine if the person at the other end of the keyboard is indeed a real jihadist, or a potential infiltrator attempting to penetrate the group.

And because online communications can be monitored, planning and coordinating attacks over the Internet or in chat rooms would be incredibly foolish behavior. It is little wonder, then, that despite their enthusiastic embrace of the Internet, al Qaeda in Iraq took that embrace only so far. They carried out these more clandestine functions the old-fashioned way: in person. Even in the 9/11 plot, when team leader Mohammed Atta needed to discuss complex and sensitive operational issues, he incurred the risks of traveling to Germany and Spain to meet with Ramzi bin al-Shibh in person rather than discuss the sensitive details on the phone or through e-mails.

There is a universe of tactical skills in which "book learning" is an important first step but will never be a viable substitute for actual practice on the street. This applies to things like weapons training and building bombs. The guidance that al Qaeda in the Arabian Peninsula has published in the online Maskaar Al-Battar magazine for using an SVD sniper rifle or a rocket-propelled grenade launcher might get someone out of the starting blocks, but there is no way to become proficient in using a weapon without actually handling one. Similarly, it is quite difficult to simply follow a recipe or written instructions and build a perfectly functioning improvised explosive device from scratch; as with any scientific endeavor, trial and error and testing in the real world usually is required. Bomb-making is a skill best learned from an experienced teacher (and many potential teachers have blown themselves up in their efforts to become bomb-building experts).

Even acquiring the necessary materials can be difficult for would-be jihadists without proper, real-world connections. Members of the alleged cell recently arrested in Toronto — now dubbed the "Canada 17" — were rounded up after they allegedly tried to buy three tons of ammonium nitrate fertilizer. Purchases of such "precursor substances" now tend to raise red flags with authorities in the Western world — a fact that highlights the difficulties of making the transition from terrorism in theory to terrorism in practice.

Unless one is content with "cyber-attacks" and hacker crimes, though, it is a necessary transition. History has shown repeatedly that, even when pre-operational planning and other activities have begun in cyberspace, jihadists conduct surveillance of their targets in the physical world as a matter of routine. From the 1993 World Trade Center bombing to the 9/11 attacks to the London bombings last July, it has been apparent that jihadists conduct not only surveillance but also dry runs of their operations when possible. They recognize, as do law enforcement agents, that however detailed a picture of a target might appear on a Web site, it is a snapshot of reality frozen in time. Successful attacks depend on knowledge of large swathes of terrain, security routines and other details that cannot be obtained from videos or photographs. Eyes-on surveillance is priceless.

The Critical Moment

Given these realities, there comes a critical moment when jihadists must abandon the cyber-world for the real world. It is at this point that many militant cells living and operating in the West have been discovered and their plots thwarted.

One reason for this is that despite the rapid and near-total embrace of technology by some jihadists, the U.S. government and its allies have been developing their signals and communications intelligence systems for a very long time now — think Bletchley Park in the 1930s and 1940s — and have a great deal of expertise and computing power at their disposal. The investigative and surveillance apparatus is not particularly nimble, but it is very effective once it has a target on which to focus.

Such targets can be provided by unwary jihadist sympathizers who visit radical Web sites, or by tips that come through foreign government liaisons. For example, in the Canada 17 case, the suspects allegedly had connections to separate cells in Britain and the United States. By working together, the British, Canadian and U.S. governments were able to mass their resources and leverage or share information. As has often been the case with investigations of organized crime groups, authorities in different jurisdictions had different pieces of the puzzle; alone, the information meant little, but when cooperating services sat down together to discuss and share information, a bigger picture emerged.

Another reason that the transition phase is so dangerous for aspiring militants has to do with the legal system in the United States and elsewhere. For example, in the United States, Britain and Canada, freedom of speech holds sway as long as suspects don't actually go so far as to encourage or order others to carry out attacks, or threaten to conduct such attacks themselves. The same thing goes for conspiracy cases (at least in the United States.) A group can conspire to carry out a violent attack as much as it wants; until an overt act is made in furtherance of that conspiracy, the suspects cannot be charged with a crime. The point at which militants leave the cyber-world and begin to take action in the real world is where they begin to make overt acts in furtherance of their conspiracy, and it is then that law enforcement agencies have the legal elements they need to make arrests, conduct searches and bring criminal charges.

In the Canada 17 case, the Royal Canadian Mounted Police (RCMP) has said publicly that it moved against the suspects at just such a critical moment: The alleged cell attempted to buy materials that could be used to manufacture explosives. To paraphrase an RCMP spokesman, the threat the suspects were believed to pose to the public, at that point, no longer was acceptable.

It is not yet clear what the future will hold for al-Zarqawi's organization in Iraq, but for the evolving generation of jihadists as a whole, past could be prologue. Ultimately, the dot-com terrorists might learn the same lessons as the dot-com entrepreneurs of the 1990s: There is no "new paradigm" in their industry. The most successful militants have recognized all along that certain basic rules — and operational practices — still apply. And for those who fail to grasp that reality, there will be a painful winnowing.

The Many Faces of Al Qaeda
July 10, 2007

With all the talk about al Qaeda "leaders," al Qaeda "factions" and militants with "links" to al Qaeda, it is useful to take a step back and clarify precisely what al Qaeda actually is. Al Qaeda is a small core group of people who share strategic and operational characteristics that set them apart from all other militants — Islamist or otherwise — the world over. All signs indicate this group is no longer functional and cannot be replicated. Whether or not Osama bin Laden is still alive, al Qaeda as it once was is dead.

Strategically, these men envisioned a world in which the caliphate would rise anew as a consequence of events they would set into motion. The chief obstacle to this goal was not the United States but the panoply of secular, corrupt governments of the Middle East. Al Qaeda knew its limited numbers precluded it from defeating these governments, so it sought to provoke the Muslim masses into overthrowing them. Al Qaeda also knew it lacked the strength to do this provoking by itself so it sought to trick someone more powerful into doing it.

By al Qaeda's logic, an attack of sufficient force against the Americans would lure the United States to slam sideways into the Middle East on a mission of revenge, leading to direct and deep U.S. collaboration with those same secular, corrupt local governments. Al Qaeda's hope was that such collaboration with the Americans would lead to outrage — and outrage would lead to revolution. Note that the 9/11 attacks were not al Qaeda's first attempt to light this flame. The 1998 U.S. embassy bombings and the 2000 USS Cole bombing were also the work of this same al Qaeda cell, but the attacks lacked the strength to trigger what al Qaeda thought of as a sufficient U.S. response.

The Real Difference

But al Qaeda is hardly the first militant group to think big. What really set al Qaeda apart was its second characteristic — its ability to evade detection. That ability was part and parcel of the way in which al Qaeda formed. Al Qaeda's roots are not merely within the various militant groups of the Arab Middle East but deep within the geopolitical struggles of the Cold War. Many of the mujahideen who relocated to Afghanistan to resist the Soviet invasion found themselves recruited and funded by Saudi intelligence, equipped and tasked by U.S. intelligence and managed and organized by Pakistani intelligence.

This exposure not only leveraged the Afghan resistance's paramilitary capabilities but also gave the mujahideen a deep appreciation for, and understanding of, the strengths and weaknesses of the U.S. and Soviet intelligence systems. When the Cold War ended, some of those mujahideen reconstituted their efforts into what came to be known as al Qaeda, and those deep understandings became part of the organization's bedrock.

Such knowledge enables al Qaeda to operate beneath the radar of nearly all intelligence agencies. It knows how those agencies collect and analyze intelligence, where the blind spots are and, most important, how long it takes for an agency to turn raw information into actionable intelligence.

This characteristic is al Qaeda's greatest asset. Al Qaeda's standards of operation assume that intelligence agencies are always waiting and watching, and only al Qaeda's understanding of those operations keeps the "base" from being busted. Operational security — not operational success — is al Qaeda's paramount concern; its attacks are meticulously planned, fantastic in scope and sacrificed in a heartbeat if the leadership suspects a breach in security. This makes al Qaeda nearly impossible to track.

It also means that al Qaeda, by necessity, is a very small, close-knit group. The organization's core — or the apex leadership, as we often call it — consists of little more than Osama bin Laden, Ayman al-Zawahiri and a double handful of trusted, heavily vetted relationships stretching back more than a decade. Disposable operatives with minimal training can be picked up for specific missions, but these people cannot do anything very complex (such as infiltrate a foreign country and hijack a civilian airliner).

Replacement of lost assets within this small group is negligible due to security concerns. Ultimately, the same security protocols that empowered al Qaeda to be a player of strategic scope are what removed al Qaeda from the chessboard.

Once the CIA and its affiliated allies named al Qaeda public enemy No. 1, al Qaeda's security instincts became its greatest liability. The rapid U.S. invasion of Afghanistan caught al Qaeda off guard — the group had assumed it would have months of U.S. pre-mission staging before the invasion, a lesson it learned from watching the first Gulf War. The quick U.S. response meant al Qaeda was forced to go into hiding before it had fully secured redundant communication, funding and travel routes. Intelligence agency efforts to penetrate al Qaeda forced the group to constrict information flow, limit financial transfers, reduce recruiting and abandon operations. Once the United States succeeded in co-opting Saudi assistance against al Qaeda in 2003 — something brought about both by a U.S. presence in Iraq and al Qaeda's own efforts to destabilize its ideological homeland — al Qaeda's star stopped falling and started plummeting.

Al Qaeda has not only failed in its attempts to trigger region-wide uprisings against the Middle East's secular governments, it has also lost the ability to launch strategically meaningful attacks — that is, attacks resulting in policy shifts by its targets. Al Qaeda can operate to a certain degree in regions where it has allies, many of whom flowed through its training camps in the 1990s, but the ability of the group that planned the 9/11 attacks to operate beyond the Middle East and South Asia seems to have disappeared. Attrition after years of confrontation with the Americans, coupled with self-imposed isolation, has rendered al Qaeda useless as a strategic actor. Not only is its ability to provide command and control nonexistent, but its self-enforced invisibility and inactivity have undermined its credibility.

Furthermore, al Qaeda has left no one truly capable of taking up its mantle. The training camps in the 1990s processed hundreds of would-be jihadists, but the quality of that training for the rank and file has been exaggerated. Most of it was a combination of poor conventional combat training and ideological indoctrination. Hence, most "veterans" of those camps have neither access to the core al Qaeda leadership nor the operational security or tactical training that would allow them to reconstitute a new elite core. They are no more members of the real "al Qaeda" than today's skinheads are members of the real Nazi party.

By the only criterion that matters — successful attacks — al Qaeda has slipped from readjusting global priorities (9/11) to contributing to the change in government of a middling U.S. ally (the March 2003 Spain attacks) to affecting nothing (the 2005 London bombings). No attacks since can be meaningfully linked to al Qaeda's control, or even its specific foreknown blessing. Al Qaeda had hoped for a conflagration of outrage that would sweep away the Middle East's political order; it managed only to raise a few sparks here and there, and now it is a prisoner of its own security.

Yet, public discussion of all things "al Qaeda," far from fading, has reached a fever pitch. But this talk — all of it — is about a fundamentally different beast.

Enter Al Qaeda the Franchise

It all started with Abu Musab al-Zarqawi, who put himself forward as the leader of the Iraqi node of al Qaeda in 2004. While one can argue that al-Zarqawi might have been through an al Qaeda training camp or shared many of bin Laden's ideological goals, no one seriously asserts he had the training, vetting or face time with bin Laden to qualify as an inner member of the al Qaeda leadership. He was a local leader of a local militant group who claimed an association with al Qaeda as a matter of establishing local gravitas and international credibility. Other groups, such as Southeast Asia's Jemaah Islamiyah, had associations with al Qaeda long before al-Zarqawi, but al-Zarqawi was the first to claim the name "al Qaeda" as his own.

For al Qaeda, prevented by its security concerns from engaging in its own attacks, repudiating al-Zarqawi would make the "base" come across as both impotent and out of touch. Accepting "association" with al-Zarqawi was the obvious choice, and bin Laden went so far as to issue an audio communiqué anointing al-Zarqawi as al Qaeda's point man in Iraq.

Others also embraced the al-Zarqawi/al Qaeda association, as dubious as it was. Al Qaeda's operational security protocols — and its ongoing presence just beyond the United States' reach in northwestern Pakistan — meant that destroying al Qaeda (the real al Qaeda) was at best a difficult prospect. But al-Zarqawi was local and active and clearly valued launching attacks over maintaining hermetically sealed security. Al-Zarqawi could be brought down. And just as al-Zarqawi's "association" with al Qaeda increased his street cred with the Arab world, that "association" also increased his value to the U.S. military as a target. Taking down an "al Qaeda-linked terrorist" was much better for purposes of public relations and funding than taking down any random militant. The media, of course, stand ready to help; reporting on a militant with direct connections to bin Laden is sexy — even if that connection was only catching a glimpse of Big "O" walking by during breakfast.

The result has been the formation of an odd iron triangle among an al Qaeda desperate for relevance, local jihadists seeking a fast track to importance and Western intelligence and law enforcement seeking credibility and funding. In the common lexicon, al Qaeda is no longer that core of highly trained and motivated individuals who tried to change the world by bringing down the World Trade Center but a do-it-yourself jihadist franchise that almost anyone can join. Some nodes are copycats who look to the real al Qaeda for inspiration; others are existing militant groups — such as Algeria's Salafist Group for Preaching and Combat, now called the al Qaeda Organization for the Countries of the Arab Maghreb — that can identify with their ideological brethren. But few to none have any real connections to al Qaeda.

Violence is certain to continue, but the lack of meaningful attacks in the West in general and the United States in particular suggests al Qaeda's degraded capacity and the West's improved security have minimized the chances of a geopolitically significant attack for the next several years.

This does not mean that would-be "al Qaeda" groups are not dangerous, or that the "war on terror" is anywhere near over. While some of the would-be al Qaeda groups almost seem comical, others are competent militants in their own right — with al-Zarqawi perhaps being the most lethal example. Their numbers are also growing. The ongoing war in Iraq has provided potential militants across the Islamic world with the motive to do something and the opportunity to gain some serious on-the-job training. Just as Soviet operations in Afghanistan created a training ground for a generation of Middle Eastern militants in the 1980s and 1990s, the Iraq war is in part a crucible for the next generation of Arab militants. Add in al Qaeda's offer of open association and we will be hearing from dozens of "al Qaedas" in the years to come.

Luckily, links between these new groups and their erstwhile sponsor are limited mostly to rhetoric. There might be a few thousand people out there claiming to be al Qaeda members, but the real al Qaeda does not exercise any control over them. They are not coordinated in their operations or even working toward a common goal. And while many of these new al Qaedas might be competent militant groups, they lack the combination of strategic vision and obsession with security that ultimately allowed the original al Qaeda to move mountains.

Top it off with terminology buy-in from Western intelligence, law enforcement and the media and the result is a war literally without end; the definition of al Qaeda is stretched by nearly any player to fit nearly any political need. The United States is now waging a war against jihadism as a phenomenon, rather than against any specific transnational jihadist movement.

Back to Square One?

The political situation in Pakistan has long imposed an unstable stasis on what many feel should have been the real focus of the war on terror all along. Since escaping from Afghanistan in 2001, the true al Qaeda has spent most of its time taking refuge in northwestern Pakistan, where a mix of political complications and ethnic and tribal allegiances have allowed it to stay out of harm's way.

The United States has been aware of al Qaeda's presence there but ultimately has not attacked for three reasons. First, al Qaeda's internal security protocols forced the organization to isolate itself. During a time when the United States had a great many fish to fry, al Qaeda seemed to have put itself into lockdown; it was issuing videos, not starting wars like Hezbollah or reconstituting like the Taliban. Second, while U.S. intelligence knows the region in which al Qaeda resides, it has never gotten enough detail to allow airstrikes to take care of business. Such not-quite-there intelligence has always been just diffuse enough to necessitate boots on the ground — and raise the specter of a disastrously botched and politically problematic military operation.

Which brings us to the third and, in many ways, most important reason for leaving al Qaeda alone. The United States felt it could not risk an assault for fear of political fallout. Ultimately, the United States needs Pakistani cooperation to wage war in Afghanistan — after all, Pakistan has the only easily traversable land border with the landlocked country — and support for radical Islam runs deep in both Pakistani society and government. So, yes, U.S. attacks against militant sites located on Pakistani soil happen all the time, but they are small pinprick operations. Any large attack could not be disavowed and, therefore, could result in the fall of the very Pakistani government that makes the hotter parts of the war on terror possible.

Back in 2005, the United States believed it had credible intelligence about a planned meeting of the core al Qaeda leadership in northwestern Pakistan. A strike force of several hundred to several thousand was assembled in order to punch through the Pakistani tribes hiding and shielding bin Laden and his allies, but the strike was ultimately abandoned because then-Defense Secretary Donald Rumsfeld felt the operation could not be kept quiet. It is one thing when Pakistanis think there are a few Americans running over the border to do something tactical. It is quite another when Pakistanis know that several thousand Americans with heavy air support are surging across to do something strategic. The U.S. might have been able to take out its target, but probably not without losing a critical ally.

Details of this attack plan were leaked July 8 to The New York Times. For us at STRATFOR, news of the plans was nothing new. It made perfect sense that this plan, and likely dozens of others like it, were at various times in the works stretching back as far as 2003 (and we have noted such on numerous occasions). What caught our attention was the timing of The New York Times article. The United States has been eyeing northwestern Pakistan for years. Why draw attention to that fact now?

The United States' core fear in 2005 was that the Pakistani government would destabilize. Well, in 2007, the Pakistani government is horrendously unstable. On July 10, Islamabad launched a multi-hour raid replete with Branch Davidian overtones against the Red Mosque complex and a gathering of radical (some would say mentally unhinged) Islamists challenging the government's writ. Be worried when the government of an Islamic republic feels it must take such action. Be doubly worried when the government taking the action already seems to be in its death throes.

Previous efforts by Pakistani President Gen. Pervez Musharraf to strengthen his political grip on the country by firing the chief justice rebounded on him so severely that he cannot even depend upon his oldest allies. Various political, military and cultural power centers are sniping at the president, making their own independent and often contradictory demands. There are also hints that Musharraf's faculties are beginning to crack. The government — as well as the president — is now teetering on the edge of oblivion, facing an unsavory menu of crushing compromise with one force or another to stay in power in name, and risking the turbulent waters of emergency rule over an increasingly hostile population.

If the threat of a government fall was the only thing holding Washington back in 2005, and now that the fall is imminent through no action of the United States, what does Washington have to gain from restraining itself any further?

This is more than a rhetorical question. The relative inactivity of al Qaeda these past six years, as well as the political situation in Pakistan, has imposed a shaky equilibrium on the issue. Al Qaeda's security protocols curtail al Qaeda's threat level, and that has allowed the United States to shelve the issue for another day. Meanwhile, the instability of Musharraf's government limits the United States' ability to pressure Islamabad over the issue of al Qaeda. Consequently, al Qaeda has been more or less hiding in plain sight.

Alter any aspect of this scenario — in this case, drastically increase the tottering of the Musharraf government — and the "stability" of the other pieces immediately breaks and the United States is forced to surge assets into Pakistan.

Washington has to assume that an al Qaeda anywhere but Pakistan is an al Qaeda that will act with less conservatism. By the American logic, al Qaeda assets in Saudi Arabia, long drilled that security is paramount, would naturally doubt that a telegram from bin Laden ordering a new attack is genuine — but they would certainly believe bin Laden himself should he show up at their door. By al Qaeda's logic, Musharraf's fall would force al Qaeda to relocate from Pakistan because the group would have to assume that the Americans would be coming.

Which means the odd stasis in the war on terror these past six years could be about to loosen up, and a front that has proved oddly cold might be about to catch fire.

The Heathrow Plot Trial: Retrospection and Implications
April 9, 2008

The trial of eight men accused of participating in a 2006 plot to bomb a series of airline flights began April 3 in London. The men are charged with conspiracy to commit murder and preparing acts of terrorism in connection with the plot, which allegedly called for using liquid explosives to bring down at least seven planes flying from London's Heathrow Airport to cities in the United States and Canada.

The trial is expected to last several months, but several interesting facts already have emerged regarding the plot and the people accused of participating in it. Although a considerable amount of media attention has been focused on the revelation that two Air Canada flights (one to Montreal and one to Toronto) were among the first seven flights targeted — the others were United Airlines flights to Washington, Chicago and San Francisco, and American Airlines flights to Chicago and New York — perhaps the most interesting revelation has been the alleged role of Mohammed Gulzar.

Gulzar reportedly flew into the United Kingdom in July 2006 using a fraudulent identity. His means of travel and his role in the conspiracy suggest he was an operational commander who had been sent from abroad to assist the grassroots plotters with their attack plans. The involvement of an operational commander sent by the al Qaeda core leadership and charged with working with grassroots operatives to orchestrate an attack is what we consider the al Qaeda 1.0 operational model.

When combined with other indicators, Gulzar's role and travel pattern seem to confirm the involvement of the al Qaeda core leadership in the plot. The participation of the core organization sheds new light on the behavior of the core al Qaeda leaders in 2006, and gives us some insight into plots they might still be planning.

Recurrent Themes

As we noted after the Heathrow plot came to light, the scheme shared several themes with other thwarted or successful al Qaeda plots, including the choice of aircraft as targets, the notion of multiple, simultaneous strikes and the use of modular improvised explosive devices, which would have been smuggled aboard the aircraft in carry-on luggage. Moreover, whoever was involved in planning the operation shared al Qaeda's penchant for "thinking big."

As originally conceived, al Qaeda's 2001 "planes operation" was to involve the simultaneous hijackings of 10 aircraft departing from both the East and West Coasts of the United States. Nine of the aircraft were to be either blown up in-flight or slammed into targeted buildings. The 10th plane was to be landed at a U.S. airport and, after all the adult male passengers were killed, a speech was to be delivered outlining al Qaeda's grievances with the United States. Al Qaeda's apex leaders — Osama bin Laden, Ayman al-Zawahiri and Mohammed Atef — eventually agreed to a scaled-down version of the planes operation involving four aircraft, which was carried out Sept. 11, 2001.

The West Coast portion of the plan was spun off as a separate operation that was to have occurred in October 2001, but which reportedly was postponed several times for various reasons. This operation, also known as the Library Tower Plot, was compromised and disrupted in 2002.

These themes also were evident in the plot to bomb American Airlines Flight 63 in December 2001. In that plan, Richard Reid successfully smuggled his "shoe bomb" aboard the aircraft. The attempt failed only because Reid tried to light the bomb's fuse in the passenger cabin (rather than a more secluded area, such as a restroom) and was stopped by a flight attendant and passengers.

The 2006 Heathrow plot, however, bears the strongest resemblance to Operation Bojinka, which Khalid Sheikh Mohammed, along with his nephew Abdel Basit, helped to plan and finance while living in Manila, the Philippines, in the mid-1990s. The tactical similarities include the targeting of multiple U.S.-flagged aircraft traveling to the United States, the use of modular explosive devices — which were to be assembled in-flight after operatives accessed their carry-on baggage — and the use of liquid explosives.

The scope of the Heathrow plot also highlights another theme common in al Qaeda plots: a tendency to think big. This theme, which was reflected in the original planes operation and in Bojinka, was also the undoing of al Qaeda attacks such as the 1993 World Trade Center bombing, the Millennium Bomb Plot and an attempted strike against the USS The Sullivans off the coast of Yemen in January 2000. Indeed, the scope of the Heathrow plot and the need to include many people in its execution is likely what opened the door for a British government informant to penetrate the group and learn of the plans.

Mohammed Gulzar

A close look at the details emerging from the trial of Gulzar and the seven other suspects also reveals other recurring themes, including the use of document fraud. Gulzar entered the United Kingdom on July 18, 2006, using a fraudulent South African passport in the name of Altaf Ravat. He reportedly was traveling with his new wife and, in order to secure a visa, alleged that he was on his honeymoon. The pair even spent a couple of days in Mauritius after leaving South Africa in order to make the honeymoon cover appear more convincing. As a British citizen, Gulzar had the right to a British passport and thus could have traveled to the United Kingdom using his own identity. The only reason to commit document fraud was to conceal his identity.

As seen in past cases involving operational commanders such as Basit and Ahmed Ressam, it is fairly common for operational commanders to commit passport fraud. In fact, recovered al Qaeda operation manuals encourage using fraudulent documents to hide one's identity, enter a country illegally or continue to stay in a country after a legitimate visa has expired. Basit had more than a dozen aliases that we know of, including the well-known fraudulent Iraqi passport in the name of Ramzi Yousef — the name by which many people still mistakenly refer to him. Gulzar's use of South Africa as a source of fraudulent documents and a transit point to Europe also exemplifies a trend we have been watching for some time now.

When British police arrested Gulzar on Aug. 9, 2006, he told them his name was Altaf Ravat and produced his South African documents. It was only after running fingerprint checks that they determined — two days after his arrest — that he really was a British citizen named Mohammed Gulzar. When questioned by police, Gulzar admitted he was not on his honeymoon, though he then said he was a missionary with the Tablighi Jamaat and was in the United Kingdom on a proselytizing mission.

As seen in past attacks — the 1993 World Trade Center bombing, the attack on the USS Cole, the East Africa embassy bombings and others that followed the al Qaeda 1.0 operational model — the operational planner does not intend to be killed or captured. He flees and lives to fight another day. In operations in which an operative plans to be killed, such as 9/11 and the July 7, 2005, London attacks, there is no need for him to hide his true identity. Gulzar's use of a fraudulent identity suggests he intended to flee after the attack. This theory is supported by the fact that British authorities recovered a number of videotapes containing the wills and suicide declarations of various members of the alleged cell, but they did not recover such a video featuring Gulzar.

Fitting the Pieces Together

Hindsight is a wonderful thing, and when we use it to plug the 2006 Heathrow plot into the big picture of al Qaeda behavior during that time, we can begin to make some assumptions as to the extent of the core leadership's involvement.

According to court testimony, the British government began to monitor many of the men allegedly involved in the plot shortly after the July 7, 2005, London attacks. It also has been reported that, like Mohammed Sidique Khan, several of the men involved in the 2006 plot had traveled to Pakistan and received training at jihadist camps. It also appears that Gulzar was sent by the core al Qaeda leadership to London in July 2006 to supervise the execution of this plot. Judging from past cases, Gulzar's preparation for the travel to London likely began several months prior to his actual arrival in the United Kingdom. Also, judging from past cases, a plan of this magnitude, involving so many aircraft, almost certainly would had to have been approved by the al Qaeda apex leadership. In all likelihood, the leadership also provided the funding for the operation, including the more than $271,000 in cash the group reportedly paid for the flat they purchased in London, where the improvised explosive mixtures were to be manufactured.

If those assumptions are indeed true, then this plot may very well be one of the operations Osama bin Laden was referring to in his Jan. 19, 2006, message when he said, "The delay in similar operations happening in America has not been because of failure to break through your security measures. The operations are under preparation and you will see them in your homes the minute they are through (with preparations), with God's permission."

The preparations for this attack also had picked up momentum by mid-2006 when the al Qaeda core leadership was undertaking what we referred to at the time as a media blitz. Indeed, just as the traffic from this blitz was beginning to slow down, As-Sahab released a video titled, "Will of the Knights of the London Raid (Part 2)," which contained the last will of London bomber Shehzad Tanweer.

This video was released one day before the anniversary of the July 7 attacks and 12 days before Gulzar arrived in the United Kingdom.

Nine days after Gulzar's arrival, and two weeks before the arrests were made, As-Sahab released a video featuring al-Zawahiri. The backdrop featured three large photographs: one of Mohammed Atef (al Qaeda's senior military chief who was killed in Afghanistan in late 2001), one of 9/11 operational commander Mohammed Atta and one of the burning World Trade Center towers.

In the video, al-Zawahiri discussed a lecture Atef gave in 2000 to al Qaeda trainees about Palestine. According to his recounting, Atta — who was among the trainees — asked, "What is the way to defeat the attack on Palestine?" Al-Zawahiri supplied his own answer in the video, saying the nation that produced the 19 "who shook America" is "capable of producing double that number."

It could be a coincidence that a large plot involving aircraft — nearly twice as many as were hijacked on 9/11 — was thwarted only two weeks after this video surfaced. But we are not big believers in coincidence — nor do we believe there are obvious (or even hidden) messages in every al Qaeda message. However, to our minds, the July 27 tape was a clear message meant to be viewed in retrospect — that al Qaeda was behind the Heathrow airline plot.

The Continuing Fixation

More than anything, the current trial is a reminder of three things. First, had the first wave of attacks successfully taken down the planes, it would have been very difficult to determine how the explosive devices had been smuggled aboard the aircraft. This means it is entirely possible the same tactic would have been used in subsequent waves of attacks.

Second, for some reason, in 2006 the al Qaeda leadership's eagerness for a spectacular attack appears to have trumped their perceived need for moderation. It was the moderation of people like Mohammed Atef that reined in the enthusiasm of the group's idealists (men such as Khalid Sheikh Mohammed) and caused them to scale down the 2001 planes operation to less than half its original size — a measure that improved operational security and assisted in the 9/11 plot's eventual success.

Finally, al Qaeda remains fixated on aircraft as targets and, in spite of changes in security procedures since 9/11, aircraft remain vulnerable to attack.

Al Qaeda and the Tale of Two Battlespaces
Oct. 1, 2008

Over the last year or so, a lot of debate has arisen over the physical strength of al Qaeda. Some experts and government officials believe that the al Qaeda organization is now stronger than at any time since the 9/11 attacks, while others believe the core organization has lost much of its leadership and operational capability over the past seven years. The wide disparity between these two assessments may appear somewhat confusing, but a significant amount of the difference between the two can be found in the fundamental way in which al Qaeda is defined as an entity.

Many analysts supportive of the view that al Qaeda has strengthened tend to lump the entire jihadist world into one monolithic, hierarchical organization. Others, like STRATFOR, who claim al Qaeda's abilities have been degraded over the years, define the group as a small vanguard organization and only one piece of the larger jihadist pie. From STRATFOR's point of view, al Qaeda has evolved into three different — and distinct — entities:

- The core vanguard group: Often referred to by STRATFOR as the al Qaeda core, al Qaeda prime or the al Qaeda apex leadership, this group is composed of Osama bin Laden and his close trusted associates. These are highly skilled, professional practitioners of propaganda, militant training and terrorism operations. This is the group behind the 9/11 attacks.

- Al Qaeda franchises: These include such groups as al Qaeda in Iraq and al Qaeda in the Islamic Maghreb (AQIM). Although professing allegiance to bin Laden, they are independent militant groups that remain separate from the core and, as we saw in the 2005 letter from al Qaeda core leader Ayman al-Zawahiri to Abu Musab al-Zarqawi, there can be a great deal of tension and disagreement between them and the al Qaeda core. These regional franchises vary in size, level of professionalism and operational capability.

- The broader grassroots jihadist movement: This group includes individuals and small cells inspired by al Qaeda but who, in most cases, have no contact with the core leadership.

Current Assessment of al Qaeda

We believe, as we did last summer, that the core al Qaeda group has weakened and no longer poses the strategic threat to the U.S. homeland that it did prior to 9/11. However, this does not mean it is incapable of re-emerging under less pressured circumstances.

On the franchise level, some groups — such as AQIM, the Yemen franchises and the franchises in Pakistan and Afghanistan — have gained momentum over the past few years. Others — such as those in Iraq, Indonesia, Saudi Arabia, the Sinai Peninsula and Morocco — have lost momentum. In our estimation, this ebb and flow has resulted in a constant threat on the franchise level, though the severity has migrated geographically as groups wax and wane in specific regions. The franchises have done little to expand their operations outside of their regions of interest and to conduct attacks against the "far enemy" — that is, attacks in the United States or Europe.

At the grassroots level, homegrown jihadists have posed a fairly consistent, though lower-level, threat. In the past, we have said that these jihadists think globally but act locally. While there are far more grassroots jihadists than there are militants in the al Qaeda franchises and vastly more than in the small al Qaeda core, the grassroots jihadists tend to be highly motivated but poorly equipped to conduct sophisticated terror attacks.

Beyond the Physical Battlefield

We believe that any realistic analysis of al Qaeda's strength must assess more than a basic head count of militants willing and able to conduct attacks. As we have noted previously, there are two battlespaces in the war against jihadism: the physical and the ideological. Although the campaign against al Qaeda has caused the core group to become essentially marginalized in the physical battlespace, the core has undertaken great effort to remain engaged in the ideological battlespace.

In many ways, the ideological battlespace is more important than the physical battlespace in the war against jihadism, and in the jihadists' war against the rest of the world. It is far easier to kill people than it is to kill ideologies. We have recently seen this in the resurgence of Bolivarian Revolution ideology in South America, despite the fact that Simon Bolivar, Karl Marx and Ernesto "Che" Guevara are long dead and buried. Ideology is the decisive factor that allows jihadists to recruit new fighters and gather funding for militant and propaganda operations. As long as the jihadists can recruit new militants, they can compensate for the losses they suffer on the physical battlefield. When they lose that ability, their struggle dies on the vine. Because of this, al Qaeda fears fatwas more than weapons. Weapons can kill people — but fatwas can kill the ideology that motivates people to fight and finance.

We are not the only ones who believe the ideological battlespace is critical. In a video released earlier this month by al Qaeda mouthpiece As-Sahab titled "The Word is the Word of Swords," one of al Qaeda's leading religious authorities, Abu Yahya al-Libi, emphasized this point from within the network.

In the video, al-Libi said the jihadist battle "is not waged solely at the military and economic level, but is waged first and foremost at the level of doctrine." He also said that his followers are in a war against an enemy that "targets all strongholds of Islam and invades the minds and ideas in the same way it invades lands and dares to destroy beliefs and meddle with the sacred things in the same way it dares to spill blood."

Interestingly, although the video recording is dedicated to detailing the preparations for the attack on the Danish embassy in Islamabad, the bulk of the 64-minute video addresses the ideological war against al Qaeda and how "true Islam" has been undermined by leaders such as King Abdullah and the Saudi religious establishment.

In an ironic twist, the progress of the combatants is easier to assess in the ideological battlespace than it is in the physical battlespace, largely because most militants plotting terror attacks try to stay invisible until they launch their operations while the ideological battle is, for the most part, conducted in plain sight.

One such visible indication on the ideological battlefield was a book written by al Qaeda's number two man, Ayman al-Zawahiri, which was released in March. The book — known as "The Exoneration" — is a long response to a book written by Sayyed Imam al-Sharif. Also known as Dr. Fadl, al-Sharif is an imprisoned Egyptian radical and a founder (with al-Zawahiri) of the Egyptian Islamic Jihad.

Published in 2007, al-Sharif's book, "Rationalizing Jihadist Action in Egypt and the World," provides theological arguments that counter many of the core jihadist teachings. Included among those teachings is the concept of takfir, or the practice of declaring a Muslim to be an unbeliever in order to justify an attack against him. Al-Sharif also spoke out against killing non-Muslims in Muslim countries and attacking members of other Muslim sects.

Al-Sharif was a significant player in the development of the jihadist theology that shaped the Egyptian Islamic Jihad (EIJ), and eventually, through al-Zawahiri and other EIJ members who became influential members of al Qaeda, al-Sharif's concepts became instrumental in shaping the ideology of jihadism as promulgated by al Qaeda. One of his books, "The Essentials of Making Ready for Jihad," was reportedly required reading for all new jihadist recruits at al Qaeda training camps in Afghanistan and Pakistan. The renunciation of jihadist ideology by such a pivotal figure was a significant threat — one serious enough to spur al-Zawahiri's refutation.

The Saudi ulema, or Muslim scholars, and former jihadist ideologues are not the only people assailing the ideology of jihadism. Western figures such as Dutch parliamentarian Geert Wilders have been highly critical of jihadism. But these outsiders have little ability to sway Muslim opinion on the street — a critical objective in fighting the ideological battle. In recent years, however, we have seen more Muslim figures speak out against jihadism, which they believe is a perversion of Islam. However, criticism is not without danger. Figures such as Egyptian political analyst Diaa Rashwan have been threatened with death because of their criticism of al Qaeda and jihadist ideology.

In addition to the previously discussed video, As-Sahab has released two other lengthy videos this month. The first, to commemorate the 9/11 anniversary, was called "The Harvest of Seven Years of Crusades." The second, called "True Imam," was released Sept. 29. Essentially, it was a tirade against the government of Pakistan and a tribute to Abdul Rashid Ghazi, who was killed in the July 2007 storming of the Red Mosque in Islamabad by the Pakistani military.

Overlap

Sometimes, things that emerge in the ideological battlespace can provide indications of important developments in the physical battlespace. For example, one of the As-Sahab videos featured clips of Mustafa abu al-Yazid (aka Sheikh Said al-Masri). An Egyptian al Qaeda military commander, al-Yazid had reportedly been killed in an Aug. 8 operation in Bajaur. But since al-Yazid makes reference in the video to the Aug. 18 resignation of former Pakistani President Pervez Musharraf, he obviously was not killed 10 days earlier.

Two others noticeably absent from these three videos were Osama bin Laden and Adam Gadahn. Bin Laden, who has not been heard from since a May 18 audio message, is once again rumored to be dead. Gadahn may also be dead, according to rumors that he was killed in a January airstrike in Pakistan's North Waziristan agency in which senior al Qaeda military commander Abu Laith al-Libi was killed. Gadahn, who has appeared in several al Qaeda video messages since emerging on the scene in 2004, has been conspicuously absent from the organization's propaganda since the January strike.

Typically, al Qaeda has been fairly forthcoming in "declaring the martyrdom" of fallen commanders like al-Libi. The death of a central figure such as bin Laden, however, could be seen as severely detrimental to the jihadist world's morale. Therefore, the group could be motivated to conceal his death. If bin Laden is still alive, however, we anticipate a message from him by the U.S. presidential elections Nov. 4, given his appearance before the 2004 presidential elections.

It would be somewhat out of character, however, for al Qaeda to avoid publicizing the death of a lesser figure such as Gadahn. With all the rumors circulating about jihadists seeking to use European-looking operatives in attacks against the West, one wonders if the silence regarding the American-born jihadist's fate is designed to keep U.S. authorities in suspense — or if it is a real indication that Gadahn is alive and has left his post in the ideological battlespace in order to go operational on the physical battlefield.

Of course, the fate of these individuals, even a central figure such as bin Laden, is not nearly as important as the fate of the ideology. And we will continue to focus on the ideological battlefield for significant developments there.

One place that needs to be watched carefully is Pakistan, where events like the Red Mosque operation and the assassination of Benazir Bhutto have potentially sown the seeds for a ripe ideological harvest for both sides. It will be important to watch and see if the Marriott bombing will, as some claimed, prove to be a watershed event that marks a change in public opinion capable of rallying popular support against the jihadist ideology in Pakistan.

CHAPTER 3: TRANSITIONS

Al Qaeda: Broader Reach and Shallower Depth
Sept. 22, 2005

As our longtime readers are likely aware, STRATFOR approaches analysis with a "net assessment" model of the world, an internal definition of how things are and the key trends driving developments at any given time. A net assessment is much more than an intuitive "gut feeling." Rather, it is the product of two key elements: a daily search for both developments that fit with the ongoing picture and anomalies that reshape it and an understanding of time, as viewed by the region or actor being assessed. And these views vary dramatically. It could be argued, for example, that an American's sense of historical cycles — which have been crammed into a national history that scarcely exceeds 200 years — is vastly different from that of the Chinese, whose civilization spans a millennium.

We apply this same perspective to al Qaeda and to attempts to understand the current status of what the Bush administration has labeled the "global war on terrorism." Given the unusual nature of this "war" against a non-state actor, there is plenty of room for debate and speculation, but in general it has been our position, from a geopolitical standpoint, that al Qaeda is losing its effectiveness as a strategic force — meaning one that is capable of drastically reshaping the behavior of nations, as it did on Sept. 11, 2001. We place emphasis on the word "strategic." We are in no way saying that al Qaeda has been conquered or declaring the United States a victor, but it is our view that a shift is occurring in the nature of the war, which is taking on more of a regional and local — rather than global — nature.

Where the U.S. calculus is concerned, this is neither unusual nor unexpected. Strategically speaking, it was to be expected that the United States would respond to the Sept. 11 attacks with all the tools in its arsenal — overwhelming military force, a heavy foreign policy stick, intelligence capabilities and law enforcement. It was also expected that, at some point, American attention would return to other issues as well — the state of the economy, an erstwhile Chinese threat, and so forth. We already have seen this happen.

But what of al Qaeda? Has its attention been diverted, its resources stretched, or its goal lines moved? Is the sense that al Qaeda is "getting the worst of it" thus far in the war — which we have stated repeatedly — actually justified?

At the tactical level, the answers to most of these questions would have to be "no." Let's dissect that for a moment, returning again to al Qaeda's core goals and to a localized understanding of time.

First, it's important to remember that — emotionalism aside — al Qaeda's core goal has not been chiefly to kill Americans or Westerners in general, but to effect political change within the Muslim world. The goal of the Sept. 11 attacks was, we have long believed, to create a sense of empowerment among the Muslim masses that would lead to popular uprisings against secular or "apostate" regimes. Whether al Qaeda actually planned to kill 3,000 people with the Sept. 11 strikes, or whether the death toll massively exceeded even its own expectations, is a matter of debate. What is known is that the attacks were, and were intended to be, "spectacular" strikes against symbolic targets that would grip the world's attention.

Second, it must be recalled that the Sept. 11 attacks were in no way the opening salvo of al Qaeda's war — simply its first success in commanding the world's attention. The war, from al Qaeda's standpoint, already had been under way for several years — likely beginning with the first bombing of the World Trade Center in 1993, or even before, perhaps with the expulsion of the Soviets from Afghanistan.

Armed with hindsight, intelligence analysts can come up with a handful of possible starting points for al Qaeda's war and track the cycles — perhaps going as far back as the assassination of Anwar Sadat in 1981 — using various rationales. But all of these cycles have one thing in common: They are long cycles, much longer than the four years that have passed since Sept. 11, 2001.

The cycle book-ended by the two strikes against the World Trade Center, in 1993 and 2001, is as useful to examine as any:

- Eight years transpired between World Trade Center I and the Sept. 11 attacks, punctuated by numerous strikes against U.S. assets overseas. These include, but certainly are not limited to, the bombings of the Khobar Towers in 1996, embassies in Kenya and Tanzania in 1998 and the USS Cole in 2000, in addition to assassination plots targeting the pope in the Philippines and against various American and British diplomats in Pakistan.

- As this list shows, many of the attacks and plots that can be identified as al Qaeda acts between 1993 and 2001 involved a "hardened target set" — military or diplomatic targets that were symbols of U.S. or Western power.

- With the Sept. 11 attacks, al Qaeda successfully struck not only at hard, symbolic targets, but at a "soft" target as well — the World Trade Center towers — and with that, the underpinnings of U.S. power: its economy.

- The tempo of al Qaeda's operations, beginning in 1993, has not slowed since Sept. 11: We have seen, for example, assassinations in Jordan (2002), brazen assaults against Westerners in Saudi Arabia (2004), deadly bombings of nightclubs and hotels in Indonesia (2003) and the Middle East (2004), and deadly bombings of passenger rail systems in Madrid (March 2004) and London, not to mention al Qaeda's obvious involvement in the insurgency in Iraq.

In short, we are seeing the natural progression of a terrorist campaign — a shift from hard targets to soft — at the tactical level, entailing both a trend toward small-scale attacks and al Qaeda's adaptation to new political and security realities.

We have seen the same progression with other groups in the past. For example, Hezbollah — under the direction of Lebanese national Imad Mughniyeh — went from the suicide bombing of U.S. Marine headquarters in Beirut in 1983 and the kidnapping and murder of CIA station chief William Buckley (who fits the definition of a "hard target") in 1984 to the bombing of a Jewish community center in Buenos Aires, Argentina, in 1994. We do not dismiss the fact that Hezbollah — which intelligence agents believe served as something of a model for the early al Qaeda and has been an ongoing target of government counterterrorism efforts — has mutated since that time to become more of a political actor, most active within its native sphere but still capable of deadly violence in many parts of the world.

From a tactical perspective, the shift to softer targets is quite worrisome — not only because they are so much more numerous than "hard" targets, but also because al Qaeda quite clearly has laid careful plans for this stage of the war.

True, the group so far has not been able to carry out a successful follow-on to Sept. 11 from U.S. soil, but that certainly is not for lack of trying. To date, U.S. intelligence agents have uncovered at least a dozen likely plots within the United States, interdicted at various stages of the attack cycle — and it is widely known that al Qaeda conducted detailed surveillance of the Citigroup building, Prudential Plaza, the New York Stock Exchange and other financial targets in New York City, as well as the World Bank and International Monetary Fund headquarters and congressional targets in Washington, D.C. From everything that U.S. intelligence knows — including information from interrogations of captured operatives — al Qaeda does not go to such lengths as sketching out the architectural weaknesses or security points of a building without eventually trying to bring it down, even when the target is known to authorities.

Now, we cannot know definitely whether al Qaeda lacks the capability to pull off another attack within the United States at this point or — for reasons of its own — has opted not to. Certainly, there have been numerous periods, such as the recent meeting of the U.N. General Assembly in New York, when the group could have made an effective statement by staging an attack — and did not. Given that, and the effectiveness of the FBI and CIA thus far in pre-empting plots, we interpret a certain amount of disruption.

In light of history, however, this analysis provides little comfort.

Though centralized command and control operations in all likelihood have been disrupted, the shift that appears to be under way — marked particularly by the Madrid and London bombings and the use of "B" team players or native-born sympathizers — is that from "al Qaeda the Organization" to "al Qaeda the Movement." We, along with government intelligence agents, have noted something of a teacher-pupil relationship in many of Ayman al-Zawahiri's video-taped statements: It is possible for al Qaeda to retroactively claim responsibility for any number of acts — independently organized and carried out by sympathizers or wannabes — thus bolstering its own credibility and that of the actors at the same time. It also is possible for al Qaeda, at times, to prove direct links between its central leadership and peripheral actors.

Tactically speaking, al Qaeda the Movement has both a broader geographic reach — drawing on regional conflicts and local grievances — and shallower depth (since it relies on small-scale strikes at softer targets) than would al Qaeda the Organization. But this is, in its own way, a strength. Given al Qaeda's sustained operational tempo since Sept. 11, 2001, it appears that the inspired movement has managed to overcome the command-and-control problem posed by the isolation and quarry status of al Qaeda's central leaders.

If you were to plot this out on a chart, what you might see are two trend lines forming an "X:" one, depicting al Qaeda's impact as a strategic force, on a declining trend; the other, depicting the tactical and security threats posed by a widespread and less visible movement, on the rise.

At this point, we find ourselves near the mid-point on the X. Al Qaeda has a top leadership that is, though in hiding, still capable of communicating with the world through broadcast recordings and the Internet, and — if London is any indication — foot soldiers around the world who are capable of flying below the radar until an attack actually is carried out. If, however, al Qaeda gels as a movement — with its ideology resonating among militants with various causes of their own — the existence or annihilation of widely recognized figureheads would be, in most respects, irrelevant.

Al Qaeda in 2006: Devolution and Adaptation
Jan. 4, 2006

The new year is an ideal time, in geopolitics as in other areas of life, to reflect on developments of the past year and, at STRATFOR, to offer our view of developments we anticipate in the realm of terrorism in 2006.

For quite some time, we have been tracking al Qaeda's metamorphosis from a relatively small group of individuals who viewed themselves as the vanguard of radical Islamism — calling themselves "Knights under the Prophet's Banner" — to a much broader movement or ideology capable of influencing the behavior of many others. The rhetoric of Osama bin Laden and the other leaders of the jihadist cause have called clearly and repeatedly for the ummah, or Islamic people, to rise up and join the "jihad against the Jews and Crusaders." While this call has not resulted in the worldwide uprising al Qaeda's leaders hoped for, it has nonetheless resonated in some quarters.

From Group to Movement

This shift from a group to a movement was evident in 2005, and we believe there will be further signs of the evolution in 2006.

In the major attacks attributed to al Qaeda or close affiliates during 2005 — such as those in London (July), Sharm el-Sheikh (July), Bali (October) and Amman (November) — operatives from regional groups, rather than teams of what might be called the "al Qaeda all-stars" that carried out the Sept. 11 operation, took up the banner of jihad. The differences here are important: The Sept. 11 hijackers were dispatched from "The Base" and came to the United States to carry out their missions. They received direct logistical support and operational guidance from al Qaeda's central command structure. On the other hand, the operatives in London and Indonesia were locals, and the operatives in Amman were regional, in the sense that they crossed over the border from Iraq to carry out their strikes.

While there are connections between the main al Qaeda leadership and operational cells in places like Britain and Iraq — as is evident from the group's statements, intercepted letters and the suicide video of London bomber Mohammed Sidique Khan — the language of the letter purportedly written by deputy al Qaeda leader Ayman al-Zawahiri to Abu Musab al-Zarqawi in Iraq clearly demonstrates that the various nodes of al Qaeda exist in more of a loose federation than a strict hierarchical chain of command. In the letter, al-Zawahiri made flattering statements to al-Zarqawi and requested that he do certain things — such as stop beheading hostages and ease his attacks against the Shia — but he was not clearly ordering him to do those things. Indeed, al-Zarqawi's militants continued to carry out attacks against Shiite targets in Iraq even after the letter was made public.

Al Qaeda's tendency to work with local militants has been well established since the early 1990s, showing up in operations targeting places like Yemen, Somalia, Ethiopia and New York. This system was institutionalized in 1998, when bin Laden issued a joint fatwa with the Egyptian Islamic Group, Al Jihad, the Jihad Movement in Bangladesh and the "Jamaat ul Ulema e Pakistan" under the name

"World Islamic Front for Jihad Against Jews and Crusaders." The fatwa declares it the "individual duty for every Muslim" to attack "Jews and Crusaders" wherever possible, "in order to liberate the al-Aqsa Mosque and the holy mosque [Mecca] from their grip, and in order for their armies to move out of all the lands of Islam."

Al Qaeda gained momentum and strength after bin Laden moved back to Afghanistan from Sudan in 1996. This enabled the group to operate without the assistance of local militants. However, after the U.S. invasion of Afghanistan in 2001, the arrests or deaths of several key al Qaeda leaders and the seizure of millions of dollars in assets, al Qaeda has reverted back to its earlier operational model.

As we have noted previously, this shift gives "al Qaeda the Movement" broader geographic and operational reach than "al Qaeda the Organization," but it is shallower in a sense: The new actor lacks the operational depth and expertise of the core group and its well-trained leadership. In fact, al Qaeda the Organization has been unable to demonstrate a continued capability to act as a strategic force — meaning one whose actions can drastically reshape the world — since the Sept. 11 attacks. There have been no strikes carried out by "all-star teams" since Sept. 11. Instead, the operations that have taken place have borne much stronger resemblances to the anti-U.S. attacks in the 1990s, such as the 1993 World Trade Center bombing or the embassy bombings in East Africa. Such actions can kill many people and are not to be lightly dismissed, but in terms of geopolitical impact and magnitude, they are mere pinpricks when compared to the stunning blow that was dealt on Sept. 11.

Thwarted Attacks, Timing and Resilience

Recently, several readers have asked whether we believe that al Qaeda has purposely avoided attacking the United States in order to play to the U.S. media and allow public opinion to turn against the war in Iraq — and, consequently, against the broader war on terrorism. The answer is no: While public opinion in the United States and elsewhere has indeed run against the war in Iraq, the lack of a successful follow-on attack by al Qaeda on U.S. soil has not been strategically planned or ordered. In other words, it has not been for a lack of trying. Since Sept. 11, U.S. intelligence and law enforcement agencies have thwarted at least a dozen likely plots against targets in the United States, interdicted at various stages of the attack cycle. In addition to the well-known plots connected to actors such as Richard Reid and Jose Padilla, it is widely known (from evidence made public in 2004) that al Qaeda conducted detailed surveillance of the Citigroup building, Prudential Plaza, New York Stock Exchange and other financial targets in New York City, as well as the World Bank and International Monetary Fund headquarters and congressional targets in Washington, D.C.

While many can and do debate tactics used by various governments in the anti-jihadist war, and we ourselves have occasionally rolled our eyes as the Pakistani government announced the arrest or death of yet another of al Qaeda's apparently limitless "number three" leaders, we must nonetheless give credit where it is due. The U.S. government and its allies have done a very good job disrupting terrorist plots and plans. The disruption strategy is really quite simple: Better to pick up an al Qaeda suspect for immigration fraud or another lesser offense than to investigate a smoking hole in the ground. There were ample instances of this tactic in play during 2005 — most notably the arrest of an imam in Lodi, California, who the FBI believes was encouraging a terrorist plot, and the arrest of an imam in Cleveland, Ohio, who is believed to be linked to a Palestinian militant group.

The trail of disrupted plots has been continuous, and it speaks to jihadists' ongoing desire to strike at the United States. Though not all of the "disrupted plots" made public by the U.S. government necessarily should be viewed as valid threats, there remains a clear record of plans to strike on U.S. soil since Sept. 11. Over the years, Islamist militants have proved to be very resilient and adaptable, and we anticipate they will continue to adapt. We note that more than eight years elapsed between the 1993 World Trade Center bombing and the Sept. 11 attacks — during which time the jihadists faced nothing approaching the level of pressure they have endured since Sept.

11 and in the ensuing "global war on terrorism." To be sure, several would-be terrorism spectaculars, such as the millennium bomb plot and Operation Bojinka, were thwarted between 1993 and 2001. It was against this backdrop of defeats that the jihadists persisted and eventually succeeded in carrying out a massive strike on U.S. soil.

Similarly, the strings of law enforcement and intelligence successes since Sept. 11 do not rule out the possibility of another strike on U.S. soil in time. We believe the likelihood of such an attack will increase as memories of Sept. 11 dim. Despite the many declarations made in the immediate aftermath of the strikes in New York and Washington that "America will never be the same," there has been a slow and steady shift back to business-as-usual and a sense of general complacency. On the whole, Americans are a people with short attention spans — and, at any rate, "alert fatigue" has always been recognized as one of the hazards of a long-term war. While we do not believe that al Qaeda is capable of carrying out another Sept. 11, that is not the same as saying they cannot carry out another strike on U.S. soil. We believe they will do so — likely with a lower impact than in 2001 — as soon as they are capable of evading pre-operational detection.

Death Toll Trends

Having said that, there is another trend to address. The shift from organization to movement may mean that al Qaeda no longer should be viewed as a strategic geopolitical force, but the jihadists are still a threat and capable of killing many people. A look at the numbers shows there have been more deaths attributed to al Qaeda in the 52 months since Sept. 11 (more than 800) than in the 52 months prior to it (less than 400) — despite the global war on terror and the successes in disrupting al Qaeda as an organization. We should note that these statistics do not include the deaths in Iraq, Afghanistan or the former Soviet Union where active insurgencies are under way, and that they do include both Western and non-Western victims. With the active resistance being fought in Iraq against coalition forces and

Iraqi civilians, the numbers of deaths caused by jihadists there would be much higher.

There are several reasons for this trend in death tolls.

First, as we have stated, al Qaeda the movement is larger and more widely dispersed geographically than al Qaeda the group. Though many of those involved in the movement may not have the training and professionalism of their "al Qaeda prime" counterparts, sheer numbers and geographic factors have allowed the movement to attack with much greater frequency and across a much broader front than the main group would be able to support. For example, in addition to the attacks in Indonesia, Britain and the Sinai Peninsula, the world witnessed the emergence of a new suicide-bombing threat from the Jamaat-ul-Mujahideen last year in Bangladesh, a region where al Qaeda the group has not historically chosen to act.

Second, there has been a shift toward soft targets. As physical security measures surrounding traditional symbols of Western power (such as the White House, the Pentagon and the U.S., British and Australian embassies) has been intensified or "hardened," the threat has been pushed toward softer target sets that are very difficult to defend, such as hotels, trains and subways. The propensity toward attacking softer targets with smaller devices to create large casualty counts was clearly delineated in Indonesia on Oct. 1, where the strike by Jemaah Islamiyah against restaurants in Bali caused more deaths than the group's last two large car-bomb attacks.

"Hard targets" are just that — hard to strike due to design and location. A large bomb is needed to penetrate defenses. However, a shift to soft targets means that small improvised explosive devices (IEDs) can be used with deadly efficiency — as actually occurred in London and Amman. The demand for resources is different as well: Scores of small IEDs can be made with the same quantity of explosives used in the 1993 World Trade Center truck bomb. Employing the "smart technology" of human bombers, who place timed or remote-detonated bombs — or themselves, in suicide mode — in ideal tactical locations, such devices very easily can kill or wound scores of people. In fact, the rail attacks in Madrid and London bore proof that small

IEDs can cause many more deaths than attacks using biological or chemical agents such as anthrax or sarin.

Thus, the U.S. government's strategy of "hardening" official sites and assets has been a double-edged sword when it comes to the private sector, particularly the transportation and hospitality industries. The public and private sectors have joined forces in efforts to protect transportation systems, but private-sector businesses like hotels and cruise lines, as well as the tourism industry in general, remain extremely difficult to secure. These targets host large numbers of "prepackaged" victims. This fact has not been obscured by the fog of war for the jihadists, who continue to target such businesses. It takes little expertise or training to place an IED on a subway or in a restaurant or hotel. We expect that jihadists will continue to exploit such vulnerabilities in the "soft target" set over the next two to three years — until there has been enough loss of life to make it a political issue for American voters. We expect this would not occur until the subways in New York City or Washington, D.C., are attacked in a London- or Madrid-style strike, the Washington-to-New York Amtrak line is hit, or there is an Amman-style suicide attack at a large U.S. hotel in a major U.S. city.

Looking Ahead

Al Qaeda remains a dangerous movement and, while it now lacks the strategic punch it carried in 2001, it will continue to attack soft targets across a large geographic front in the coming year. We expect that in 2006, strikes will be carried out in both the traditional hotspots and in areas not previously known for Islamist militant activity. The active armed struggles in Iraq, Afghanistan and the Caucasus continue to act as a kind of "jihadist war college," and as the graduates of that school return to their countries of origin, they will continue to share their training and experience with militants back home. The connections that the militants make in places like Iraq and Chechnya also will link them to the global movement in the same way that the jihad in Afghanistan did for the preceding generation.

It is not certain what the new year will bring for al Qaeda the group. It is not clear at this point that bin Laden is even alive — he has not been heard from in more than a year, and there have been no conclusive signs of his survival since we pondered in September that he might indeed be dead. However, we are certain that whatever elements of the organization remain are dedicated to striking the United States as hard and as frequently as they are able. Given their past plots and interrogations of key players such as Khalid Sheikh Mohammed, we know that al Qaeda the group has been interested for years in striking financial targets, aircraft and chemical and petroleum plants. Because al Qaeda has a demonstrated history of revisiting targets after failed or foiled attacks, it is logical that they will continue to attempt strikes against such targets in the future.

Bin Laden's notable absence during the past year has underscored al Qaeda's shift from organization to movement — and indicates that even when he is not seen to be in control the movement keeps steaming right along. And this suggests that if bin Laden is alive and eventually is taken out by the United States, the movement will continue. Ideologies are much harder to kill than individuals.

That brings us to another key point: There has been a gradual but accelerating decline in support for the ideology of jihadism in the Muslim world. Though pockets of staunch support for jihadism remain, the tide of public opinion has begun to turn against al Qaeda and jihadism in some crucial locations, including Saudi Arabia. Al-Zawahiri himself has acknowledged defeat in Saudi Arabia, where the monarchy has persuaded the masses to turn against jihadists — or "deviants," as they are termed by the regime.

It is this kind of ideological battle that must be fought and won to defeat jihadism. It is indeed a long-term war, and we do not anticipate its conclusion in 2006.

The Next Phase of Evolution?
June 8, 2006

Canadian authorities recently arrested 17 men, accusing them of planning terrorist attacks after some members of the group bought what they believed to be some 3 tons of ammonium nitrate fertilizer, which can be used to make explosives. The men allegedly were planning attacks against symbolic targets in Toronto and Ottawa in a plot that reportedly included bombings, armed assaults and beheadings.

One of the things that make this case interesting is that the group — now dubbed by the media as the "Canada 17" — reportedly had connections to alleged jihadists in other countries, whose earlier arrests were widely reported. Those connections included two men from the United States — Ehsanul Islam Sadequee and Syed Haris Ahmed — who reportedly traveled from Georgia in March 2005 to meet with Islamist extremists in Toronto. Authorities have said they conspired to attend a militant training camp in Pakistan and discussed potential terrorist targets in the United States. There also is said to be a connection to a prominent computer hacker in Britain who was arrested in October and charged with conspiring to commit murder and cause an explosion.

The June 2 arrests certainly underscore the possibility that Canada, which has a long history of liberal immigration and asylum policies, has been used by jihadists as a sanctuary for raising funds and planning attacks. But the most intriguing aspect of the Canada case is that it seems to encapsulate a trend that has been slowly evolving for some time. If the allegations in the Canada 17 case are at least mostly true, it might represent the emergence of a new operational model for jihadists — an "al Qaeda 4.0," if you will.

In other words, the world might be witnessing the emergence of a grassroots jihadist network that both exists in and has the ability to strike in multiple countries — without support or oversight from the central al Qaeda leadership.

A History of Operational Models

To understand what we mean by "al Qaeda 4.0," let's review the history of operational models that al Qaeda has used over the years. The first identifiable operational model — the 1.0 — was that used in the early 1990s. This model revolved around Osama bin Laden, the "Afghan Arabs" or veterans of the Soviet resistance in Afghanistan, and formal militant training camps. In this iteration, operational commanders trained at camps in Afghanistan — most notably Khalden — received funding and logistical support from bin Laden and others, and conducted operations in various parts of the world.

We do note that this is a rather controversial starting point for our history. It can be credibly argued (and indeed, we have had such arguments at STRATFOR) that this phase represents a kind of "proto-al Qaeda" — that al Qaeda had not been established as a formal organization in the early 1990s and, as a result, any attacks during that period were not carried out by a centralized organization that was controlled by bin Laden. The contrasting point of view is that al Qaeda actually did exist at that time, but because bin Laden was living as a guest in Sudan (and then, later, in Afghanistan), he did not claim responsibility for the attacks or plots that were carried out at that stage, so as not to bring political pressure (or military retaliation) against his host governments.

Be that as it may, the model (which for purposes of this analysis will be called "1.0") was evident in many jihadist operations of the early 1990s: A succession of individuals who went forth from bin Laden-run training camps to plan and conduct attacks elsewhere. These men frequently connected with veterans of the Afghan jihad — or with others who had passed through the training camps in Afghanistan — once they arrived in the target country and, thus, operational cells were born.

One prime example of this 1.0 model can be seen in the plots of Abdel Basit and Ahmed Ajaj, who left the Khalden training camp and flew to New York in September 1992. Ajaj was arrested for a passport violation, but Basit entered the country and went on to orchestrate the 1993 World Trade Center bombing. The operational model also applies in the 1992 strikes in Yemen against the U.S. Embassy in Sanaa and U.S. Air Force personnel in Aden, and in plots that did not come to fruition — for example, Operation Bojinka and Abdel Basit's plots to kill Pope John Paul II and U.S. President Bill Clinton.

A slight variation on this model emerged in the later 1990s. Operational commanders with more obvious links to al Qaeda and bin Laden were dispatched to Yemen, Canada, Kenya and other countries to establish cells and carry out attacks. This 1.1 model could be seen in the 1998 bombings of U.S. embassies in Kenya and Tanzania, the disrupted "millennium bomb plot" and the attack on the USS Cole in 2000. At this stage, bin Laden was still denying involvement in such attacks.

The 2.0 operational model is the easiest to recognize, but thus far it appears to have been used only on 9/11: An al Qaeda "all-star team" was selected, trained and dispatched by the central leadership to the target country to carry out an attack. Bin Laden's stance on claims of responsibility shifted following that event. For months, he continued to deny al Qaeda's involvement, but over time came to acknowledge it and — quite recently — stated outright that he personally oversaw all the details.

The handpicked operatives used for 9/11 or any other attack under this model would be, by definition, better trained than the ad hoc operatives behind the version 1.0 and 1.1 attacks — and roughly equal in stature to the 1.0 commanders. For the most part, the all-star teams appear to have practiced better operational security than their forebears as well — though, not being supermen, they did make some tradecraft mistakes.

This model provides both tactical advantages and disadvantages for the host organization. On the upside, it allows for excellent command and control of the operation. On the downside, it is a resource-intensive model; numerous operatives are required, as is a facility for training and a command structure capable of staying in communication with the agents in the field and providing them with logistical support. Given the clues uncovered after 9/11 and the efforts of the United States and other countries to disrupt such infrastructure, it is currently very difficult for al Qaeda to employ this model. This, in turn, led to a devolution of sorts for the organization and the adoption of a third operational model.

The 3.0 model — which applies to most of the attacks attributed to al Qaeda since 9/11 — involves "grassroots jihadists." By this, we mean cells with a local leadership carrying out attacks in a country with which they have a long association — rather than commanders or groups of operatives who are deployed by the central al Qaeda command for purposes of conducting a strike in a foreign country. In some cases, it appears that members or leaders of these cells have been trained at terrorist camps or fought in a jihad somewhere, but they are, for the most part, citizens who have been inspired by al Qaeda, and the cells have done their recruiting locally. Moreover, they choose targets and conduct operations only in the countries where they live.

Examples of this model might be found with al Qaeda in the Arabian Peninsula and Egypt's Tawhid wa al-Jihad, the group that has claimed recent attacks against tourist targets in the Sinai Peninsula. It appears al Qaeda 3.0 operatives lack the skill and operational savvy of their 2.0 counterparts; they have a tendency to make operational errors that lead to thwarted plots and arrests.

It is possible, but not a prerequisite, within the 3.0 model that operatives have contact with the central organization. Mohammed Sidique Khan, believed to have been the leader of the cell that carried out multiple bombings in London in July 2005, apparently had some contact with al Qaeda in Pakistan. Nevertheless, this organizational structure differs significantly from the 1.0 and 2.0 models in that the operational commander and/or attack team is not dispatched by the al Qaeda leadership to another country for purposes of an operation.

Interestingly enough, al Qaeda has claimed many, if not most, of the attacks that fall under the 3.0 model — even though the leadership was, by definition, far less involved in the planning and execution of such operations than of others that it denied.

Al Qaeda 4.0?

It is within this context that the unfolding case in Canada is most significant. As details emerge, it is becoming apparent that those arrested would — if the allegations are true — represent a grass-roots cell. Authorities say they have found no evidence linking the suspects to the central al Qaeda leadership. However, it also would seem that the men went beyond the 3.0 model of thinking and acting locally. Given the links to suspects in the United States (Sadequee and Ahmed) and to operatives in Britain, there is reason to believe that they might have been part of an international network of local cells — or grassroots groups that "think globally and act locally," to borrow a phrase.

The implication here is one of expanded capabilities. A 3.0 operation would be, for all intents and purposes, fairly isolated: jihadists striking at local targets within their reach, with existing means. A 4.0 operation could entail more sophisticated levels of coordination — and the possibility of simultaneous strikes against geographically diverse targets (for instance, London, Toronto and New York). Previously, such a feat could have been accomplished only by the core al Qaeda organization. For a grassroots network to accomplish that feat, without direct involvement from the central leadership, would represent a generational leap forward in jihadist operations.

The Internet seems to be an important factor fostering the emergence of such a loose but cohesive structure. Of course, personal relationships are still important. In the case in question, Sadequee — who lived in Canada before moving to the United States — is the pivotal figure. He and Ahmed — who are charged with having videotaped potential targets in the Washington, D.C., area — are said to have met during 2005 with men Sadequee knew from his time in Canada, and three of those men were among the 17 rounded up last week. But the Internet is a great facilitator of communications as well. Since 9/11, chat rooms and Web sites have experienced a surge in popularity among jihadists. They provide a great forum for like-minded people to connect. Indeed, technology is not necessarily verboten for the current generation of jihadists, Islamist principles notwithstanding; another of the suspects connected to the Canada case is a computer hacker and "cyberwarrior" from Britain, Younis Tsouli, who goes by the handle "Irhabi007."

Significantly, the Internet can be an Achilles' heel for jihadist networks. It gives authorities a way of identifying people who may have become radicalized and a means to monitor their behavior — both virtual and physical — and communications. Authorities also can establish and nurture relationships with suspected militants online, much as they frequently impersonate children on the Internet in efforts to catch pedophiles.

Law enforcement and intelligence agencies also might find it possible to infiltrate militant cells or recruit sources within certain communities in order to disrupt attack plans. This option is particularly viable when a cell is extremely large, like the 17-man group in Canada. That said, it also can be difficult to identify and target cells effectively, particularly when authorities are dealing with a large universe of potential suspects.

Case Study Notes

As a tactical case study, the events in Canada offer up several other operational lessons. One intriguing point is that, according to the allegations, the cell continued to move ahead with plans for attacks, even after contacts in other countries had been arrested. Tsouli and some of his associates were taken into custody in October 2005; the arrests of Ahmed (in the United States) and Sadequee (in Bangladesh) followed in March and April of this year. Moreover, the indictments in the U.S. case, which were widely reported in the U.S. and Canadian press, noted that Ahmed and Sadequee had traveled to Canada in March 2005 to meet with suspects who were being actively investigated at that time.

Now, conventional wisdom would dictate that any cells in operational mode would go underground when their associates started getting rounded up, and attempt to keep their noses clean until after the heat was off. But the allegations in the Canada case would indicate that conventional wisdom held no sway: The cell members kept plugging right along with their plans regardless. From a law-enforcement and intelligence standpoint, this underscores the need for continued vigilance after a plot seemingly has been thwarted; Letting down one's guard and assuming the danger has passed is not an option, since other plots in the pipeline might not necessarily have been shelved. This, however, is not an entirely new lesson. Similar cycles were evident in 1993 — a group of conspirators who had been tied to the World Trade Center bombing cell attempted to attack other targets in New York City a few months afterward — and in 2005, with the botched public transit bombings only two weeks after the July 7 attacks.

Separately, one must note that most of the suspects in the Canada 17 case were very young — too young to have fought jihad in places like Afghanistan or Bosnia, as had many of the Version 1.0 operatives. Thus, the emerging 4.0 structure, with its affinity for the Internet, might be a natural result of "Generation Y" jihadists seeking to create an infrastructure.

As a follow-on to that, many of the Canadian suspects reportedly became radicalized in a short time after 9/11. This radicalization process also has been observed with grassroots operatives in London and elsewhere in the recent past. We are reminded here that al Qaeda, like the violent anarchists of the 19th century, aptly might refer to its attacks as "propaganda of the deed." Among its primary objectives in carrying out the 9/11 attacks was sending a message of empowerment to the Muslim people and sparking a general uprising that would culminate in the rebirth of the caliphate. While the envisioned uprising did not materialize, it has become increasingly obvious that al Qaeda's message of empowerment and the call to jihad has resonated strongly with some people.

Another objective of 9/11 was to spark an American retaliation — a goal in which al Qaeda obviously succeeded. The U.S. invasions of Afghanistan and Iraq have been viewed by many in the Muslim world as aggression against Islam, and for grassroots militants (especially those of Generation Y) this is reason enough to act. The passions of these young jihadists have been further enflamed by their views of the Israeli/Palestinian dynamic and events in other parts of the Muslim world. They feel a driving need to do something about perceived aggression against fellow Muslims, even if they do not care about the goal of re-establishing the caliphate. This is a different genre of rational actors. They realize that their attacks are not likely to contribute to the revival of Muslim political power; they act instead out of anger and vengeance.

Thus far, operational security (OPSEC) has been the bane of the grassroots jihadists. Many suspected cells, including the one in Canada, have been disrupted as a result of poor OPSEC. However, due to the sheer numbers of fish in the pond, and the many ways of blending in or escaping notice, it is hard for authorities to identify and monitor all of these individuals, even when they make mistakes. Some inevitably will slip through the cracks. It also must be remembered that, controversial ideologies aside, many of these people are highly intelligent and well educated. Some are bound to study and learn from the mistakes made by their predecessors — and evolve into smarter fish.

At the very least, the evolutionary cycle — catching up ever-younger generations of jihadists — is yet another solid indication that jihadism will linger even if the leadership of the al Qaeda organization is located and destroyed. Ideology is much harder to kill than individuals, and this particular ideology now appears to have taken root among Muslim populations stretching from London, Ontario, to London, England, to Lahore. The emergence of Generation Y militants indicates that the problem is not likely to disappear completely.

Finally, the ability of grassroots cells to network across international boundaries, and even across oceans, presents the possibility that al Qaeda 4.0 cells could, now or in the future, pose a significant threat even without a central leadership structure — meaning, a structure that can be identified, monitored and attacked. If these grassroots organizations begin to improve their OPSEC practices, the risk they represent will increase. This very well could become the dominant operational model for the foreseeable future.

Al Qaeda in 2007: The Continuing Devolution
Dec. 28, 2006

The theme of STRATFOR's 2006 forecast for al Qaeda and the jihadist movement centered on the evolution — or the devolution, really — from al Qaeda the group to a broader global jihadist movement. This essentially was a shift from an al Qaeda operational model based on an "all-star team" of operatives who are selected, trained and dispatched to the target by the central leadership to an operational model that encourages independent "grassroots" jihadists to conduct attacks, or to a model in which al Qaeda provides operational commanders who organize grassroots cells. We refer to this shift as devolution because what we are seeing now is essentially a return to the pre-9/11 model.

This shift has provided "al Qaeda the Movement" broader geographic and operational reach than "al Qaeda the Organization." This larger, dispersed group of actors, however, lacks the operational depth and expertise of the core group and its well-trained terrorist cadre.

The metamorphosis continued in 2006, with al Qaeda announcing the merger of existing jihadist groups such as Gamaah al-Islamiyah (GAI) in Egypt and Algeria's Salafist Group for Preaching and Combat (GSPC) and others in the Maghreb into their global jihadist umbrella organization. These groups have had long-standing links to al Qaeda, and the announcement of the mergers is really a formalization of the relationship, though these new nodes joined al Qaeda's formal network of affiliate groups in Iraq, Saudi Arabia, the Sinai Peninsula and Afghanistan.

Since the announcements, these new groups have not yet demonstrated that they are capable of boosting al Qaeda's operational effectiveness. We have seen no attacks that can be attributed to GAI, and perhaps the only attacks that can be attributed to the GSPC are the Dec. 11 attack against a bus carrying foreign oil workers and the simultaneous Oct. 30 attacks against two police stations in Algeria. Given this lack of results, the announcements ring somewhat hollow, as the mergers have not given al Qaeda the surge of momentum it might have wanted.

The major attacks in 2006 in Abqaiq, Saudi Arabia; Dahab, Egypt; Dubba and Marib, Yemen; and Damascus, Syria, were all conducted by existing regional nodes and not the main al Qaeda organization. These attacks did show a broad geographic reach stretching across the Middle East but, except for the Dahab attack, they were essentially all failures.

Overall, 2006 was not a good year for the al Qaeda nodes in Saudi Arabia and the Sinai. It also was a dismal year for the Iraq affiliate, whose charismatic leader Abu Musab al-Zarqawi was killed in June. Twelve months have made a vast difference in the fortunes of the Iraq node. Last year at this time, al-Zarqawi made the headlines almost daily and his organization was conducting frequent and spectacular attacks. Now, following the death of al-Zarqawi, al Qaeda in Iraq has been largely marginalized and eclipsed by Iraqi Sunni and Shiite insurgent groups.

Going into 2007, we anticipate a continuation of this shift toward a movement — though it will be important to watch for any signs of operational activity by al Qaeda the group, as opposed to its prodigious public relations efforts.

The Shift to Soft Targets

As we noted in January, the shift to the broader movement model allowed for an increase in the number of attacks, although the movement's lack of expertise was forcing it to focus its attacks against soft targets such as hotels, trains and subways. This shift resulted in a larger numbers of casualties than the more spectacular attacks against hardened targets. Indeed, the casualty count from jihadist attacks in

111

2005 - 2006 ATTACKS

DATE	TYPE	PLACE	TARGET	KILLED
03-19-05	Car bomb	Doha	Theater	2
04-07-05	Suicide bomber	Cairo	Tourists/Bazaar	3
04-30-05	Attempted suicide bombing	Cairo	Tourists/Museum	3 (attackers only)
07-11-05	Suicide bombings	London	Subway/Bus	56
07-21-05	Attempted suicide bombing	London	Subway/Bus	0
07-23-05	Suicide bombing	Sharm al Sheikh	Tourist resort	88
08-19-05	Rocket attack	Aqaba	US Navy warship	1
10-01-05	Suicide attacks	Bali	Tourists/Restaurants	26
11-09-05	Suicide bombings	Amman	Hotels	60
02-24-06	Assault/Car bomb	Abqaiq	Oil facility	4
03-02-06	Car bomb	Karachi	US Diplomat	4
04-24-06	Suicide bombing	Dahab	Tourist resort	24
04-26-06	Suicide bombings	Sinai	Multinational observers	2 (bombers only)
09-12-06	Assault/Car bomb	Damascus	US Embassy	4 (3 attackers)
09-15-06	Assault/Car bomb	Yemen	Oil facilities	5 (4 attackers)
12-10-06	Roadside bomb	Algeria	Bus of oil industry workers	1

the 52 months following 9/11 was more than double that of the 52 months prior — and those numbers would be vastly increased if the deaths in Iraq and Afghanistan were included.

However, not as many attacks occurred in 2006 as we anticipated. In fact, the number of attacks and the casualties they generated were down for 2006. In many cases, such as Damascus, Abqaiq and Yemen, the attacks resulted in the deaths of more attackers than victims, and the only attack to produce a sizable death toll was in Dahab, where 24 people died. This trend in which attacks against tourist targets in Egypt produce the deadliest jihadist attack of the year continued from 2005, when the attack in Sharm el-Sheikh, Egypt, killed 88 people. (Incidentally, that represents not only far more victims than in the Dahab attack but also more victims than all of the 2006 attacks combined.) When Sharm el-Sheikh is combined with the 2005 attacks in Bali, Amman and London, jihadist militants produced far more deaths in 2005 than in 2006. (These statistics do not include attacks conducted in war zones or areas of insurgency such as Iraq, Afghanistan, Israel/Palestine, Chechnya/Russia, Sri Lanka or Kashmir/India.)

The only jihadist strike against a hardened target in 2006 was the failed attack against the U.S. Embassy in Damascus in September. A car bombing was directed against an employee of the U.S. Consulate in Karachi, Pakistan, but that attack happened a block away from the hardened facility. It was, however, the only one of the two to produce an American death.

Target Sets

As we said in January, al Qaeda the group has long been interested in striking financial targets, aircraft and chemical and petroleum plants. Because of that, and al Qaeda's demonstrated history of revisiting targets after failed or foiled attacks, it was logical to project that it would continue to attempt strikes against such targets in 2006.

The petroleum sector indeed was targeted in 2006, as the strikes against petroleum facilities in Abqaiq and Yemen, and against oil contractors in Algiers, demonstrate. Although no attack occurred against financial targets as we anticipated, we still believe that target set remains at risk for the future, along with the others.

Although authorities thwarted the plot to simultaneously destroy several airliners en route from London to the United States, it once again demonstrated that al Qaeda and the jihadist movement maintain a significant interest in airline targets. Details released in February on the Library Tower bombing plot provide another example of this fixation.

Disruption Strategy Continues

Once again, there has been no successful attack on U.S. soil in 2006 — though the thwarted airliner plot was definitely aimed at the United States. Likewise, the anticipated attacks in European locations such as the United Kingdom, Denmark, France and Italy failed to materialize — again, not for lack of trying on the part of the jihadists.

The U.S. government and its allies have been successful over the past year in disrupting terrorist plots and plans in many locations. The strategy of disruption these countries are following is really quite simple: It is better to pick up an al Qaeda suspect on immigration fraud or another lesser offense than to investigate a smoking hole in the ground. Although there has been significant skepticism over the terrorist credentials of those responsible for some of these plots, such as the one involving the self-styled jihadist cell known as the Miami Seven, the plots serve as a reminder that there are people who remain committed to striking the United States. Over the years, Islamist militants have proved to be resilient and adaptable in the face of adversity, and they will certainly continue to adapt.

It is important to remember that more than eight years elapsed between the 1993 World Trade Center bombing and the 9/11 attacks — during which time al Qaeda and its jihadist network faced nothing approaching the level of pressure they have endured since then. There were several thwarted terrorist spectaculars between 1993 and 2001, and yet the jihadists persisted and eventually succeeded in carrying out a massive strike on U.S. soil.

Therefore, the string of law enforcement and intelligence successes since 9/11 does not rule out the possibility of another strike on U.S. soil in time. We believe the likelihood of such an attack will increase as memories of 9/11 dim and the public grows weary of the inconvenience and financial burden of increased security measures.

The Jihadist 'War College'

The forecast, which noted that the active armed struggles in Iraq, Afghanistan and the Caucasus still serve as a kind of "jihadist war college," predicted that its graduates would continue to share their training and experience upon returning to their countries of origin.

We already have seen a transfer of terrorism tactics and technology to Afghanistan, and we anticipate that this will continue in the future. In addition, the interpersonal connections that the militants make in places such as Iraq and Chechnya also will link them to the global movement in the same way the jihad in Afghanistan did for the preceding generation.

Al Qaeda as a Strategic Threat to the U.S. Homeland
July 25, 2007

The July 17 release of portions of a National Intelligence Estimate (NIE) titled "The Terrorist Threat to the U.S. Homeland" has generated a great deal of comment from STRATFOR readers, many of whom contend it is at odds with our assessment published shortly before the contents of the NIE were leaked. In that report, we attempted to clarify what we mean when we refer to "al Qaeda" and we differentiate between the small al Qaeda core organization (what we call "al Qaeda prime"), the somewhat wider array of al Qaeda franchise organizations (such as al Qaeda in Iraq) and the broad

115

assortment of grassroots jihadists who have no actual connection to the core organization. Our assessment also echoed an assertion we have been making for quite some time now — that al Qaeda lacks the ability to pose a strategic threat to the United States.

It must be understood that al Qaeda and other jihadists still pose a tactical threat to the U.S. homeland. In other words, they can still kill Americans. In fact, in looking at the jihadist shift in operations abroad, attacks against smaller, softer targets have actually caused more fatalities than large-scale strikes against hard targets. However, attacks against low-level soft targets, such as the November 2005 hotel attacks in Amman, Jordan, and the July 7, 2005, suicide bombings in London, do not have the strategic impact of a 9/11-style attack.

A number of tactical and strategic considerations have led us to conclude that al Qaeda does not pose a strategic threat.

Tactical Realities

As long as the ideology of jihadism exists and jihadists embrace the philosophy of attacking the "far enemy," they will pose a threat on U.S. soil. Though the U.S. government has tightened visa and asylum restrictions since 9/11, those processes still contain holes. Furthermore, given that even small, repressive regimes have been unable to control their immigration, it is not surprising that a country as large as the United States, one that must deal with the open nature of U.S. society, cannot hermetically seal its borders to prevent terrorist operatives from entering. Jihadist operatives still can reach the United States illegally by committing immigration fraud or slipping across the border. Legally, they can obtain visas, be from visa-waiver countries or be U.S. citizens. Of course, people residing in the United States who decide to "go jihad" also pose a threat. While some, perhaps even most, of these jihadist operatives will be caught before they can enter, some inevitably will get into the country. There undoubtedly are such people — both transnational and homegrown operatives — in the United States right now. That is a tactical reality.

Another tactical reality is that the U.S. government simply cannot protect every potential target. While insights gained from al Qaeda's targeting criteria have helped U.S. authorities protect high-value targets, there simply are far too many potential targets to protect them all. The federal government might instruct state and local authorities to protect every bridge, dam, power plant and mass-transit system in their jurisdiction, but the reality on the ground is that there are not nearly enough resources to protect them all, much less every shopping mall, state fair, Jewish Community Center, football game or other potential soft target where people concentrate.

Another tactical consideration is the ease with which an attack can be conducted. As Virginia Tech shooter Cho Seung Hui and D.C. sniper John Allen Muhammad demonstrated, it is not difficult to kill people. In fact, Cho killed more people with handguns in his attack at Virginia Tech than Jemaah Islamiyah killed in Jakarta, Indonesia, in the August 2003 bombings of the Marriott Hotel and the Australian Embassy combined. University of Oklahoma student Joel Henry Hinrichs also demonstrated the ease with which someone can fabricate an improvised explosive device (IED) using triacetone triperoxide (TATP) without being detected.

Given this reality and the fact that jihadists are committed to staging attacks on U.S. soil — and are willing to die in the process — it really is rather astounding that we have not seen more jihadist attacks in the United States.

Strategic Considerations

There are, however, some strategic considerations that help explain why we have not seen al Qaeda prime execute the long-expected follow-on attack. The first is that strategic attacks are difficult to pull off. A strategic attack is one that results in a significant geopolitical policy shift by its target. An attack that destroys a strategic-level target such as the U.S. Capitol or that causes mass casualties — kills 1,000 or more people — would certainly rise to this level.

One problem is that most strategic targets are large, well constructed and hard to destroy. In other words, just because a strategic target is attacked does not mean the attack has succeeded. Indeed, many such attacks have failed. Even when a plot against a strategic target is successfully executed, it might not produce the desired results and therefore would be considered a failure. For example, despite the detonation of a massive truck bomb in a parking garage of the World Trade Center in 1993, the attack failed to achieve the jihadists' aims of toppling the two towers and producing mass casualties or of causing a major U.S. foreign policy shift.

Many strategic targets also are well protected against conventional attacks. Their large standoff distances protect them from vehicle-borne improvised explosive devices, while this security measure and others make it difficult to cause significant damage to them using smaller IEDs or small arms.

To overcome these obstacles, jihadists have been forced to look at alternate means of attack. Al Qaeda's use of large, fully fueled passenger aircraft as guided missiles is a great example of this, though it must be noted that once that tactic became known, it ceased to be viable — as Flight 93 demonstrated. There is little chance that a flight crew and passengers of an aircraft would allow it to be seized by a small group of hijackers now. However, concern remains over the possible use of large cargo aircraft or even some of the larger general aviation aircraft in this fashion — especially given al Qaeda prime's fixation on aviation.

There also has been a major strategic shift in the way al Qaeda and jihadists are viewed. Prior to 9/11 they were considered more or less a nuisance and little attention was paid to them. They operated from safe and relatively comfortable bases in Afghanistan and were able to train and dispatch operatives abroad with ease. They also were able to take ready advantage of the global financial system to transfer money, and they were able to hold "regional conferences" in places such as Kuala Lumpur, Malaysia. In fact, we know that prior to 9/11 al Qaeda was planning a number of strikes at the same time, including the follow-on plot to attack the Library Tower and other West

Coast targets with aircraft, and a plot to attack U.S. Navy targets in Singapore that was put on hold so it did not interfere with the success of the 9/11 operation. With all that surveillance and planning going on, it is no wonder the 9/11 Commission Report called the summer of 2001 "The Summer of Threat." Since 9/11 and the launching of the "global war on terrorism," however, the U.S. government's anti-terrorism tool kit has been turned against the organization in full force.

Although no strategic attacks have occurred since 9/11, it is not for lack of trying on the jihadists' part. Indeed, many attempts have been discovered and thwarted. While the United States and its allies were not really focused on the al Qaeda threat prior to 9/11, they are almost over-focused on the threat today, labeling even grassroots wannabe jihadists like the Miami Seven as al Qaeda. Still, this intense focus, the policy of disrupting plots and the increase in public awareness have made it more difficult for jihadists to operate in the United States today.

As we said, U.S. authorities will not be able to stop every attack — and they know the next attack is a matter of when and not if. Because of this, they have taken great pains to attempt to limit the impact the long-expected attack will have. They have done this by raising awareness about the items that can be used in terror attacks and by limiting access to these items. Today, when a gasoline tanker truck goes missing, a quantity of dynamite is stolen from a quarry or a suspicious person attempts to buy a quantity of ammonium nitrate fertilizer, people quickly report these incidents and alerts are issued. This simply did not happen prior to 9/11.

Another factor is public reaction. The American public was shocked by 9/11. Not only by the scope and devastation of the attack, but by the very fact it happened. Prior to 9/11, Americans considered terrorism as something that happens "over there" and not at home. Today, the American public has been anticipating a follow-on attack on the U.S. homeland since the minute the towers fell. This means that when the next attack happens, there will be sadness, anger and a healthy round of political finger-pointing — but it will not come as a surprise.

Unconventional Weapons

Al Qaeda also has considered overcoming security measures to launch strategic strikes by using chemical, biological, radiological or nuclear weapons (CBRN). We know al Qaeda has developed crude methods for developing chemical and biological weapons. It also is possible al Qaeda prime was behind the anthrax mailings in 2001. However, as STRATFOR has repeatedly pointed out, chemical and biological weapons are expensive, are difficult to use and have proved to be largely ineffective in real-world applications. A comparison of the Aum Shinrikyo chemical and biological attacks in Tokyo with the March 2004 jihadist attacks in Madrid clearly demonstrates that explosives are far cheaper, easier to use and more effective at killing people. The failure by jihadists in Iraq to use chlorine effectively in their attacks also underscores the problem of using improvised chemical weapons.

Of course, it is not unimaginable for al Qaeda or other jihadists to think outside the box and attack a chemical storage site or tanker car, using the bulk chemicals to attack another target — much as the 9/11 hijackers used aircraft as the means to attack the end target. However, while such an attack could release enough of a deadly chemical to kill many people, most people would be evacuated before they could receive a lethal dose, as past industrial accidents have demonstrated. Therefore, such an attack would be messy but would be more likely to cause panic and mass evacuations rather than mass casualties.

The same can be said of a radiological dispersion device (RDD), sometimes called a "dirty bomb." While RDDs are easy to deploy — so simple that we are surprised one has not already been used against the U.S. homeland — it is very difficult to immediately administer a lethal dose of radiation. Therefore, the bomb part of a dirty bomb would likely kill more people than the device's "dirty," or radiological, component. However, use of an RDD would result in evacuations and could require a lengthy and expensive decontamination process. Because of this, we refer to them as "weapons of mass disruption" rather than weapons of mass destruction.

The bottom line is that a nuclear device is the only element of the CBRN threat that would create mass casualties and guarantee the success of a strategic strike. Al Qaeda, however, would find it very difficult to obtain (or manufacture) such a device while it is under the intense pressure it faces today. If the organization had possessed such a device since before 9/11, as some have claimed, we believe operatives would have used it long before now.

The Al Qaeda Shell

Clearly, jihadists want to hit the U.S. homeland. In fact there has not been a time in the last 10 to 15 years when some jihadist somewhere hasn't been plotting to attack the United States. There likely are homegrown and transnational jihadists in the United States right now plotting attacks. There also are a wide variety of vulnerable targets in the United States and, as we have said, attacking them is not that difficult.

We believe the United States is long overdue for a jihadist attack. Like U.S. Homeland Security Secretary Michael Chertoff, we believe the elements are likely in place for such an attack in the near future. However, we do not believe the attack will be of the same magnitude as the 9/11 attacks.

The problem for al Qaeda is that the core group, in the words of the NIE, is "likely to continue to focus on prominent political, economic and infrastructure targets with the goal of producing mass casualties, visually dramatic destruction, significant economic aftershocks and/ or fear among the U.S. population." It is one thing to launch an attack against the Sears Tower, for example; it is quite another thing to succeed in bringing it down. We believe al Qaeda can attack a target like the Sears Tower, but our assessment is that the organization currently lacks the ability to launch a devastating strategic attack — one that would destroy the target.

Does this mean al Qaeda will lack this capability forever? No. If the United States and its allies were to cease pressuring the organization, and the jihadist movement as a whole, it could in time regenerate the capability. However, we disagree with the NIE assertion that the group already has regenerated to that point. Al Qaeda prime is still dangerous at the tactical level, but strategically it is only a shell of its former self.

Summer 2007: The Attack that Never Happened
Oct. 17, 2007

The summer of 2007 was marked by threats and warnings of an imminent terrorist attack against the United States. In addition to the well-publicized warnings from Homeland Security Secretary Michael Chertoff and a National Intelligence Estimate that al Qaeda was gaining strength, a former Israeli counterterrorism official warned that al Qaeda was planning a simultaneous attack against five to seven American cities. Another warning of an impending dirty bomb attack prompted the New York Police Department to set up vehicle checkpoints near the financial district in Lower Manhattan. In addition to these public warnings, U.S. government counterterrorism sources also told us privately that they were seriously concerned about the possibility of an attack.

All these warnings were followed by the Sept. 7 release of a video message from Osama bin Laden, who had not been seen on video since October 2004 or heard on audio tape since July 2006. Some were convinced that his reappearance — and his veiled threat — was the sign of a looming attack against the United States, or perhaps a signal for an attack to commence.

In spite of all these warnings and bin Laden's reappearance — not to mention the relative ease with which an attack can be conducted — no attack occurred this summer. Although our assessment is that the al Qaeda core has been damaged to the point that it no longer poses a strategic threat to the U.S. homeland, tactical attacks against soft targets remain simple to conduct and certainly are within the reach of jihadist operatives — regardless of whether they are linked to the al Qaeda core.

We believe there are several reasons no attack occurred this summer — or since 9/11 for that matter. Before we discuss these factors, though, we must note that the lack of an attack against the U.S. homeland since 9/11 has not been the result of a calculated decision by bin Laden and the core al Qaeda leadership. Far too many plots have been disrupted for that to be the case. Many of those foiled and failed attacks, such as the 2006 plot to destroy airliners flying from London to the United States, the Library Tower Plot, Richard Reid's failed attempt to take down American Airlines flight 63 in December 2001 and Jose Padilla's activities, bear connection to the core al Qaeda leadership.

So, if the core al Qaeda has desired, and even attempted, to strike the United States, why has it failed? Perhaps the greatest single factor is attitude — among law enforcement and intelligence agencies, the public at large, the Muslim community and even the jihadists themselves.

Law Enforcement and Intelligence

Prior to the 1993 World Trade Center bombing, the FBI denied the existence of an international terrorism threat to the U.S. homeland, a stance reflected in the bureau's "Terrorism in the United States" publications in the late 1980s and early 1990s. Even after the radical Zionist Rabbi Meir Kahane was killed by a jihadist with connections to the Brooklyn Jihad Office and "Blind Sheikh" Omar Abdul-Rahman, the FBI and Department of Justice denied the act was terrorism and left the investigation and the prosecution of the gunman, ElSayyid Nosair, to New York police and the Manhattan District Attorney's Office (although they were greatly aided on the federal level by the Diplomatic Security Service, which ran investigative leads for them in Egypt and elsewhere).

It was only after Nosair's associates detonated a large truck bomb in the parking garage of the World Trade Center in 1993 that the existence of a threat to the United States was recognized. Yet, even after that bombing and the disruption of other plots — the July 1997 plot to bomb the New York subway system and the December 1999 Millennium Bomb Plot — the apathy toward counterterrorism programs remained. This was most evident in the low levels of funding and manpower devoted to counterterrorism programs prior to 9/11. As noted in the 9/11 Commission Report, counterterrorism programs simply were not a priority.

Even the April 1995 Oklahoma City bombing made no real difference. Some changes were made, such as physical security enhancements at federal buildings, but they were merely window dressing. The real problems, underlying structural problems in the U.S. government's counterterrorism efforts — resources, priorities and intelligence sharing — were not addressed in a meaningful way.

Prior to 9/11, experts lecturing to law enforcement and intelligence groups about the al Qaeda/transnational terrorist threat to the United States were met with indifference. Of course, following 9/11 some of those same groups paid careful attention to what the experts had to say. Transnational terrorism had become real to them. The 9/11 attacks sparked a sea change in attitudes within law enforcement and intelligence circles. Counterterrorism — aggressively collecting intelligence pertaining to terrorism and pursuing terrorist leads — is now a priority.

Citizen Awareness

Before the 1993 World Trade Center bombing, the American public also was largely unconcerned about international terrorism. Even after that bombing, most Americans remained apathetic about the terrorist threat to the U.S. homeland. This was partly the result of the media's coverage of the 1993 bombing, which seemed to focus on the hapless, bumbling Mohamed Salameh and not the cunning and dangerous Abdel Basit (who is more widely known by his alias, Ramzi Yousef). Furthermore, the follow-on plot to that attack, the 1993 New York bomb plot — for which Abdul-Rahman and some of his followers were accused of planning strikes against the Lincoln Tunnel and other New York City landmarks — was thwarted. This led many to believe that the government had a handle on terrorism and that the United States was protected from such attacks. The second plot was thwarted before it could be executed, and most Americans never saw the gigantic crater (nearly 100 feet across) that the February 1993 truck bomb created through several floors of Building One's reinforced concrete parking garage. Instead, they saw only a bit of smoke billowing from the damaged building. The 1993 cases lacked the stunning visual displays of the 9/11 attacks.

The events of 9/11 also created a 180-degree change in how people think about terrorism and how they perceive and respond to suspicious activity. "If you see something, say something" has become a popular mantra, especially in New York and other large cities. Part of this stems from the changed attitudes of law enforcement officials, who not only have issued appeals in the press but also have made community outreach visits to nearly every flight school, truck driving school, chemical supply company, fertilizer dealer and storage rental company in the United States. Through media reports of terrorist plots and attacks, the public also has become much more aware of the precursor chemicals for improvised explosive mixtures and applies far more scrutiny to anyone attempting to procure them in bulk.

U.S. citizens also are far more aware of the importance of preoperational surveillance and — fair or not — it is now very difficult for a person wearing traditional Muslim dress to take a photograph of anything without being reported to the authorities by a concerned citizen.

This change in attitude is particularly significant in the Muslim community itself. Contrary to the hopes of bin Laden — and the fears of the U.S. government — the theology of jihadism has not taken root in the United States. Certainly there are individuals who have come to embrace this ideology, as the arrests of some grassroots activists demonstrate, but such people are very much the exception. In spite of some problems, the law enforcement community has forged some strong links to the Muslim community, and in several cases Muslims have even reported potential jihadists to law enforcement. Even in places where jihadism has more successfully infiltrated the Muslim community, such as Europe, North Africa and Saudi Arabia, the jihadists still consider it preferable to wage the "real" jihad against "crusader troops" in places such as Iraq, rather than to attack soft civilian targets in the West or elsewhere. As unpopular as it is to say, in many ways Iraq has served as a sort of jihadist magnet, drawing young men from around the world to "martyr" themselves. Pragmatically, every young jihadist who travels from Europe or the Middle East to die in Baghdad or Ar Ramadi is one less who could attack Boston, London, Brussels or Rome.

Attitude is Everything

In late 1992 and early 1993, amateur planning was all that was required to conduct a successful terrorist attack on U.S. soil. In addition to the almost comical mistakes made by Salameh, serious gaffes also were made by Ahmed Ajaj and Basit as they prepared for the 1993 World Trade Center bombing. However, because of the prevailing apathetic attitude among law enforcement officials and the public in general, those mistakes were not fatal to the operation.

Given the changes in attitude since 9/11, however, no operation conducted as poorly as the 1993 bombing would succeed today. Before the bombing, the FBI investigated the cell that carried it out, made the determination that the men were harmless fanatics and closed the investigation. That would not happen today, as even slightly goofy, wannabe terrorists such as the Miami Seven are vigorously investigated and prosecuted when possible.

When Ajaj and Basit flew into JFK Airport in September 1992, authorities pretty much ignored the fact that Ajaj was found transporting a large quantity of jihadist material, including bomb-making manuals and videos. Instead, he was sentenced to six months in jail for committing passport fraud — a mere slap on the wrist — and was then to be deported. Had authorities taken the time to carefully review the materials in Ajaj's briefcase, they would have found two boarding passes and two passports with exit stamps from Pakistan. Because of that oversight, no one noticed that Ajaj was traveling with a companion. Even when his co-conspirators called Ajaj in jail seeking his help in formulating their improvised explosive mixtures and recovering the bomb-making manuals, the calls were not traced. It was not until after the bombing that Ajaj's involvement was discovered, and he was convicted and sentenced.

These kinds of oversights would not occur now. Furthermore, the attitude of the public today makes it far more difficult for a conspirator like Nidal Ayyad to order chemicals used to construct a bomb, or for the conspirators to receive and store such chemicals in a rented storage space without being reported to the authorities.

Another change in attitude has been on the legal front. Prior to the 1993 World Trade Center bombing, there were no "terrorism" statutes concerning the use of weapons of mass destruction or acts of terrorism transcending national borders. Instead, prosecutors in terrorism cases struggled to apply existing laws. The defendants in the 1993 New York bomb plot case were not charged with conspiring to build bombs or commit acts of international terrorism. Rather, they were convicted on "seditious conspiracy" charges. Similarly, Salameh was convicted of violating the Special Agricultural Worker program and with damaging U.S. Secret Service cars stored in the basement of the World Trade Center building.

The U.S. security environment has indeed improved dramatically since 1993, largely as a result of the sweeping changes in attitude, though also to some extent because of the magnet effect of the war in Iraq. Success can engender complacency, however, and the lack of attacks could allow attitudes — and thus counterterrorism resources — to swing back toward the other end of the spectrum.

Iraq: The Upcoming Jihadist Exodus
Dec. 4, 2007

The top jihadist leader in Iraq called Dec. 4 for a fresh bombing campaign against Iraqi security forces. In a 42-minute audio message, which surfaced on the Internet, Islamic State of Iraq leader Abu Omar al-Baghdadi said every soldier in his group must explode at least three bombs by the end of January. He further said the attacks should target the "unbelievers who wear uniforms and all those who fight alongside the occupiers." Al-Baghdadi announced the formation of a special unit, the al-Sidique Brigade, which is tasked with attacking Sunni tribal militia aligned with the U.S. military against the jihadists.

The message comes on the heels of significant — perhaps devastating — jihadist losses and a serious decline in their operational capability in recent months. Therefore, it suggests the jihadists not only are on the defensive, but also are getting quite desperate over seeing their sphere of operations shrink in Iraq. The Iraqi node of al Qaeda and its local allies, including the Islamic State of Iraq, know their future in Iraq is limited for four reasons: there is a Shiite majority in the country, the sectarian strife the jihadists triggered remains within acceptable levels, Sunnis have turned against them en masse and a U.S.-Iranian understanding is making progress. Therefore, while stirring the Iraq pot as much as possible, they also must be working on an exit strategy, which entails relocating to other countries.

The available options include Saudi Arabia, Syria, Jordan and Kuwait — all of which to one extent or another facilitated the flow of jihadists into Iraq. In the case of the Saudis, Jordanians and Kuwaitis, it was meant to counter the rise of the Shia and Iran after the collapse of the Baathist regime. However, the states always intended this flow to be one-way and would not want to see a repeat of what happened after the Soviets left Afghanistan and the Islamist militants returned to their home countries to wreak havoc. But the question is whether these states can prevent the jihadists from returning.

Complicating this issue is the desire on the part of the Arab states (with the exception of Syria) to prevent Iran from consolidating its influence in Iraq, especially after the recent U.S. National Intelligence Estimate. That report will likely lead to an understanding between the United States and Iran — one that would institutionalize Shiite dominance in Iraq, something every Sunni Arab state fears.

While the Arab states do not want militants to operate on their respective soils, they do want to harness them as a tool to counter Iran and the Shia. Similar to the Pakistanis' ambivalent take on jihadists, the Arabs — especially the Saudis — are unsure how to achieve both goals.

This is a very serious dilemma for the Saudis, who are caught between a rock and a hard place — not just at the state level. Even within society, the tug of war between those calling for reforms and those trying to limit the reforms is making it more difficult to determine a position on dealing with the jihadists. For now, both Riyadh and Islamabad must determine how to keep the rogue elements separate from those they still can control. There also are some in both states who are calling for a complete end to the flirtation with the jihadists.

The Syrian government also has been making use of jihadists in the Lebanese context, though Damascus will have a hard time cooperating with the United States and Iran on Iraq while continuing to deploy Sunni Islamist militants in Lebanon. In the process, the government is likely to get burned at home.

Jihadists fleeing Iraq also could seek to relocate their operations to Afghanistan/Pakistan, Central Asia or North Africa. Quite a few Libyans and Algerians went to fight in Iraq, for example. The return of these jihadists, however, could pose a threat to ongoing moves by Tripoli and Algiers to open up their respective energy sectors for Western investment. The fear of attacks, instability and economic damage will prompt many Arab/Muslim states to try to block the flow of fleeing fighters from Iraq.

It is too early to say whether these efforts will succeed. However, in the post-9/11 global security environment — which limits the jihadists' freedom of movement — these relocations will not rise up to the levels seen from Afghanistan in 1989 or even in 2001.

Al Qaeda in 2008: The Struggle for Relevance
Dec. 19, 2007

On Dec. 16, al Qaeda's As-Sahab media branch released a 97-minute video message from al Qaeda second-in-command Ayman al-Zawahiri. In the message, titled "A Review of Events," al-Zawahiri readdressed a number of his favorite topics at length.

This video appeared just two days after As-Sahab released a 20-minute al-Zawahiri message titled "Annapolis — The Treason." In that message, al-Zawahiri speaks on audio tape while a still photograph of him is displayed over a montage of photos from the peace conference in Annapolis, Md. As the title implies, al-Zawahiri criticizes the conference.

Although the Dec. 14 release appeared first, it obviously was recorded after the Dec. 16 video. Given the content of the Dec. 14 message, it most likely was recorded shortly after the Nov. 27 Annapolis conference and before the Dec. 11 twin bombings in Algeria. The two latest releases are interrelated, however, given that the still photo of al-Zawahiri used in the Dec. 14 message appears to have been captured from the video released two days later.

After having been subjected to two hours of al-Zawahiri opinions in just two days, we cannot help but wonder whether anyone else is listening to this guy — and, if so, why? This question is particularly appropriate now, as we come to the time of the year when we traditionally prepare our annual forecast on al Qaeda. As we look ahead to 2008, the core al Qaeda leadership clearly is struggling to remain relevant in the ideological realm, a daunting task for an organization that has been rendered geopolitically and strategically impotent on the physical battlefield.

Devolution

The theme of our 2007 al Qaeda forecast was the continuation of the metamorphosis of al Qaeda from a smaller core group of professional operatives into an operational model that encourages independent "grassroots" jihadists to conduct attacks, or into a model in which al Qaeda provides the operational commanders who organize grassroots cells. We referred to this shift as devolution because it signified a return to al Qaeda's pre-9/11 model.

We noted that the shift gave "al Qaeda the Movement" a broader geographic and operational reach than "al Qaeda the Organization," but we also said that this larger, dispersed group of actors lacked the operational depth and expertise of the core group and its well-trained terrorist cadre.

Looking back at the successful, attempted and thwarted attacks in 2007, this prediction was largely on target. The high-profile attacks and thwarted attacks were plotted by grassroots groups such as the one responsible for the attacks in London and Glasgow, Scotland, or by regional affiliates such as al Qaeda's franchise in Algeria, al Qaeda in the Islamic Maghreb (AQIM). The core al Qaeda group once again failed to conduct any attacks.

British authorities have indicated that the men responsible for the failed London and Glasgow attempts were linked in some way to al Qaeda in Iraq, though any such links must have been fairly inconsequential. The al Qaeda franchise in Iraq has conducted hundreds of successful bombings and has a considerable amount of experience in tradecraft and bomb making, while the London and Glasgow attempts showed a decided lack of tradecraft and bomb-making skills.

Regional Franchises

The al Qaeda nodes in Egypt, the Sinai Peninsula and Indonesia were all quiet this year. The Egyptian node has not carried out a successful attack since announcing its allegiance to al Qaeda in August 2006. Jemaah Islamiyah, al Qaeda's Indonesian franchise, has not

131

conducted a successful attack since the October 2005 Bali bombing, and the Sinai node, Tawhid wa al-Jihad, did not conduct any attacks in 2007. Its last attack was in April 2006.

The Saudi franchise conducted only one successful operation in 2007, a small-arms attack against a group of French and Belgian nationals picnicking near Medina, which resulted in the deaths of four Frenchmen. This is a far cry from the peak of its operational activities during the summer of 2004. The Yemen node also conducted one attack, as it did in 2006, a July 2 suicide car bombing against a tourist convoy that resulted in the deaths of eight Spaniards. The Moroccan element of AQIM attempted to carry out attacks in March and April, though the group's inept tactics and inadequate planning resulted in the deaths of more suicide bombers than victims.

These regional nodes largely have been brought under control by a series of successful campaigns against them. Police operations in Saudi Arabia, the Sinai and Indonesia have provided some evidence that the groups have been trying to regroup and refit. Therefore, the campaigns against these regional nodes will need to remain in place for the foreseeable future to ensure that these organizations do not reconstitute themselves and resume operations.

We noted in our 2007 forecast that AQIM had not yet proven itself. However, the series of attacks by AQIM this year demonstrated that the group is resourceful and resilient, even in the face of Algerian government operations and ideological divisions. In fact, AQIM was the most prolific and deadly group in 2007 outside of the active war zones of Iraq and Afghanistan. With al Qaeda in Iraq facing serious problems, AQIM is in many ways carrying the torch for the jihadist movement. With other regional nodes seemingly under control, the U.S. and other governments now can pay more attention to AQIM. Throughout the coming year, the Algerian government likely will receive much more assistance from the United States and its allies in its efforts to dismantle the group. AQIM — the former Salafist Group for Preaching and Combat (GSPC) — has existed since the early 1990s and its dedicated cadre has survived many attempts to eliminate it, though it likely will be pressed hard over the next year.

In a Nov. 3 audio message, al-Zawahiri said the Libyan Islamic Fighting Group (LIFG) had formally joined the al Qaeda network. This came as no real surprise, given that members of the group have long been close to Osama bin Laden, and al Qaeda has a large number of Libyan cadre, including Abu Yahya al-Libi, Anas al-Libi and Abu Faraj al-Libi (who reportedly is being held by U.S. forces at Guantanamo Bay, Cuba). The LIFG-al Qaeda link became apparent in September 2001, when the U.S. government identified the LIFG as a specially designated terrorist entity (along with the GSPC and others).

Although Libyans have played a large role in al Qaeda and the global jihadist movement, the LIFG itself has been unable to conduct any significant attacks. Historically, Libyan security forces have kept the LIFG in check to the point that most high-profile Libyan jihadists operate outside Libya, unlike the AQIM leadership, which operates within Algeria. It will be important to watch this new node to see whether it can ramp up its capabilities to conduct meaningful operations inside Libya, or even in other countries where the group has a presence — though we doubt it will be able to pose a serious threat to the Libyan regime.

Another relatively new jihadist presence appeared on the radar screen Feb. 13, when the Fatah al-Islam group bombed two buses in the Lebanese Christian enclave of Ain Alaq, killing three people. Following the Lebanese army's efforts to arrest those group members believed responsible for the bombing, the group holed up in the Nahr el-Bared refugee camp in northern Lebanon, where it endured a siege by the Lebanese army that began in March and lasted until early September. Shaker al-Abssi, the leader of Fatah al-Islam, is said to have links to former al Qaeda in Iraq leader Abu Musab al-Zarqawi. Along with al-Zarqawi, al-Abssi was sentenced to death in Jordan for his suspected involvement in the 2002 killing of U.S. diplomat Laurence Foley in Amman. He served a three-year jail sentence in Syria and then moved into Nahr el-Bared to establish Fatah al-Islam, which is believed to be controlled by Syrian intelligence. While Fatah al-Islam lost many of its fighters during the five-month siege, we have

133

received intelligence reports suggesting that the Syrians are helping the group recover. The intelligence also suggests that the more the Syrians cooperate with U.S. objectives in Iraq, the more they will press the use of their jihadist proxies in Lebanon. In pursuing such a course, the Syrians are playing with fire, which may well come to haunt them, as it has the Saudis and Pakistanis.

Iraq's Contribution

Events in Iraq likely will have a significant impact on the global jihadist movement in the coming year. Since the death of al-Zarqawi, al Qaeda in Iraq's operational ability steadily has declined. Furthermore, the organization appears to be losing its support among the Iraqi Sunnis and apparently has had problems getting foreign fighters into the country as of late. This could indicate that there will soon be an exodus of jihadists from the country. These jihadists, who have been winnowed and hardened by their combat against the U.S. military, might find the pastures greener in the countries they enter after leaving Iraq. Like the mujahideen who left Afghanistan following the Soviet withdrawal, they could go on to pose a real threat elsewhere.

Additionally, since 2003 Iraq has been a veritable jihadist magnet, drawing jihadists from all over the world. If there is no possibility of seeking "martyrdom" in Iraq, these men (and a few women) will have to find another place to embrace their doom. The coalition's list of foreign jihadists killed in Iraq shows that most of the fighters have come to the country from places such as Saudi Arabia, Algeria and Morocco, but jihadists also have come from many other countries, including the United States, United Kingdom and European Union. Jihadists in these places might opt to follow the example of the July 2005 London bombers and martyr themselves in their countries of residence.

Jihadists in Iraq have had the luxury of having an extensive amount of military ordnance at their disposal. This ordnance has made it relatively simple to construct improvised explosive devices, including large truck bombs. This, in turn, has made it possible to engage hard targets such as U.S. military bases and convoys. Jihadists without access to these types of weapons (and the type of training they received in Iraq) will be more likely to engage soft targets. In fact, the only group we saw with the expertise and ordnance to hit hard targets outside of Iraq and Afghanistan in 2007 was AQIM. As we forecast for 2006 and 2007, we anticipate that the trend toward attacking soft targets will continue in 2008.

Afghanistan and Pakistan

Despite U.S. and NATO forces' repeated tactical victories on the battlefield, al Qaeda's Afghan allies, the Taliban, continue to survive, which is the critical task for any guerrilla force engaged in an insurgent war. Following a pattern that has been repeated many times throughout Afghan history — most recently in the war following the Soviet invasion — the Taliban largely seek to avoid extended battles and instead engage in hit-and-run guerrilla operations. This is because they realize that they cannot stand toe-to-toe with the superior armaments of the foreign invaders. Indeed, when they have tried to stand and fight, they have taken heavy losses. Therefore, they occasionally will occupy a town, such as Musa Qala, but will retreat in the face of overwhelming force and return when that superior force has been deployed elsewhere.

Due to the presence of foreign troops, the Taliban have no hope of taking control of Afghanistan at this juncture. However, unlike the foreign troops, the Taliban fighters and their commanders are not going anywhere. They have a patient philosophy and will bide their time until the tactical or political conditions change in their favor. Meanwhile, they are willing to continue their guerrilla campaign and sustain levels of casualties that would be politically untenable for their U.S. and NATO rivals. The Taliban have a very diffuse structure, and even the loss of senior leaders such as Mullah Dadullah and Mullah Obaidullah Akhund has not proved to be much of a hindrance.

Just over the border from Afghanistan, Pakistan has witnessed the rapid spread of Talibanization. As a result, Islamabad now is fighting a jihadist insurgency of its own in the Federally Administered Tribal Areas and North-West Frontier Province. The spread of this ideology beyond the border areas was perhaps best demonstrated by the July assault by the Pakistani army against militants barricaded inside the Red Mosque in Islamabad. Since the assault against the mosque, Pakistan has been wracked by a wave of suicide bombings.

Pakistan should be carefully watched because it could prove to be a significant flash point in the coming year. As the global headquarters for the al Qaeda leadership, Pakistan has long been a significant stronghold on the ideological battlefield. If the trend toward radicalization continues there, the country also could become the new center of gravity for the jihadist movement on the physical battlefield. Pakistan will become especially important if the trend in Iraq continues to go against the jihadists and they are driven from Iraq.

The Year Ahead

Given the relative ease of getting an operative into the United States, the sheer number of soft targets across the vast country and the simplicity of conducting an attack, we remain surprised that no jihadist attack occurred on U.S. soil in 2007. However, we continue to believe that the United States as well as Europe remain vulnerable to tactical-level jihadist strikes — though we do not believe that the jihadists have the capability to launch a strategically significant attack, even if they were to employ chemical, biological or radiological weapons.

Jihadists have shown a historical fixation on using toxins and poisons. As STRATFOR repeatedly has pointed out, however, chemical and biological weapons are expensive to produce, difficult to use and largely ineffective in real-world applications. Radiological weapons ("dirty bombs") also are far less effective than many people have been led to believe. In fact, history clearly has demonstrated that conventional explosives are far cheaper, easier to use and more effective at killing people than these more exotic weapons. The failure by jihadists in Iraq to use chlorine effectively in their attacks has more recently underscored the problems associated with the use of improvised chemical weapons — the bombs killed far more people than did the chlorine they were meant to disperse as a mass casualty weapon.

Al-Zawahiri's messages over the past year clearly have reflected the pressure that the group is feeling. The repeated messages referring to Iraq and the need for unity among the jihadists in the country show that al-Zawahiri believes the momentum has shifted in Iraq and things are not going well for al Qaeda there. Tactically, al Qaeda's Iraqi node still is killing people, but strategically the group's hopes of establishing a caliphate there under the mantle of the Islamic State of Iraq have all but disappeared. These dashed hopes have caused the group to lash out against former allies, which has worsened al Qaeda's position.

It also is clear that al Qaeda is feeling the weight of the ideological war against it — waged largely by Muslims. Al-Zawahiri repeatedly has lamented specific fatwas by Saudi clerics declaring that the jihad in Iraq is not obligatory and forbidding young Muslims from going to Iraq. In a message broadcast in July, al-Zawahiri said, "I would like to remind everyone that the most dangerous weapons in the Saudi-American system are not buying of loyalties, spying on behalf of the Americans or providing facilities to them. No, the most dangerous weapons of that system are those who outwardly profess advice, guidance and instruction..." In other words, al Qaeda fears fatwas more than weapons. Weapons can kill people — fatwas can kill the ideology that motivates people.

There are two battlegrounds in the war against jihadism: the physical and the ideological. Because of its operational security considerations, the al Qaeda core has been marginalized in the physical battle. This has caused it to abandon its position at the vanguard of the physical jihad and take up the mantle of leadership in the ideological battle. The core no longer poses a strategic threat to the United States in the physical world, but it is striving hard to remain relevant on the ideological battleground.

In many ways, the ideological battleground is more important than the physical war. It is far easier to kill people than it is to kill ideologies. Therefore, it is important to keep an eye on the ideological battleground to determine how that war is progressing. In the end, that is why it is important to listen to hours of al-Zawahiri statements. They contain clear signs regarding the status of the war against jihadism. The signs as of late indicate that the ideological war is not going so well for the jihadists, but they also point to potential hazards around the bend in places such as Pakistan and Lebanon.

Afghanistan, Pakistan: The Rhetoric of a Bin Laden Tape
March 20, 2008

The CIA confirmed March 20 that an audio message attributed to al Qaeda leader Osama bin Laden posted on the Internet on March 19 is authentic. A U.S. intelligence official could not, however, confirm when the message was recorded. In the unusually short message addressed to Europeans, the chief of the global jihadist network attacks the West for publishing drawings of the Prophet Mohammed deemed offensive to Muslims.

Bin Laden makes a number of key points, including accusing Pope Benedict XVI of playing a key role in instigating a new crusade against Muslims in the form of the insulting drawings of Mohammed. The al Qaeda leader says that by insulting the prophet, the West has abandoned all morals and etiquette of conflict, describing it as worse than killing Muslim civilians.

The jihadist leader also attacks Saudi King Abdullah for not putting an end to the situation despite his alleged ability to do so given that the king forced the British government to open an investigation into the embezzlement of billions in the al-Yamamah arms deal. Bin Laden also refers to former British Prime Minister Tony Blair as the new representative of the Middle East Quartet, helping date the message. He concludes his message with a warning that if the West does not stop insulting Mohammed, it should be prepared for a response from the jihadist movement.

Though he addresses the West, bin Laden's target audience is the Muslim world. Support there for jihadists has suffered a significant decline over the last few years, but anti-Western sentiment remains high. Though the tape seeks to exploit the cartoon issue to reverse this waning support for jihadism, it probably will not have much impact beyond the limited segment of the Muslim world that remains sympathetic to the jihadist cause.

Nothing about the contents of the tape proves it was made recently. Everything bin Laden discusses is old news, meaning this probably is an older tape that only now has surfaced. The delay between production and broadcasting suggests that the communications system has suffered a decline, as some previous tapes reached the public domain within a week of their production.

Only three bin Laden videos have emerged since his late 2001 disappearance from Tora Bora. His other recordings have been either audiotapes or videos containing voice messages over old images of the al Qaeda leader. Intriguingly, after a flurry of mostly video communiqués from bin Laden's deputy, Ayman al-Zawahiri, during 2005-2006, the jihadist No. 2 also stopped issuing tapes. Meanwhile, other al Qaeda members like al-Qaeda ideologue Abu Yahya al-Libi and the group's U.S. operative, Adam Gadahn, have appeared in videos. This anomaly underscores al Qaeda's vulnerability.

The latest communiqué validates what STRATFOR has been saying for some years now, namely, that the jihadists have ceased to be a strategic threat to the United States. Though they remain a tactical threat, the reversal of their fortunes in Iraq means they are geographically limited to Afghanistan and Pakistan, where the global jihadist leadership is based and al Qaeda and the Taliban are demonstrating their operational prowess. While attacks in the West, especially Europe, remain a possibility, the jihadists have threatened Europe for four years. Apart from the Madrid and London bombings, they have not demonstrated the ability to make good on their threats.

The Insignificance of Bin Laden's Latest Message
Jan. 14, 2009

In his first audio message since May 2008, al Qaeda leader Osama bin Laden issued an audio recording through As-Sahab, al Qaeda's media arm, on Jan. 14. The message consisted of statements about the ongoing Israeli operation in Gaza and warnings to U.S. President George W. Bush's successor about the challenges of inheriting the wars in Iraq and Afghanistan. In the message, bin Laden focuses on Bush and his cooperation with Israel in its operation against Hamas in the Gaza strip, and he urges Muslims to support the mujahideen with "money and men." He goes on to link the world's economic troubles to the United States' missions in Iraq and Afghanistan, saying that if the next U.S. president "withdraws from the war, that would be a military defeat, and if he goes on with it, he'll drown in economic crisis."

Bin Laden and the core al Qaeda leadership (what we call al Qaeda prime) do not matter much anymore, beyond their symbolic power. The continual release of statements without attacks means that these tapes are falling on deaf ears. Al Qaeda prime has failed to pull off an operation since the London bombings in 2005 — and even that attack appears to have involved only a tangential link to the grassroots jihadist network behind the plot. Even in South Asia, where al Qaeda is active, it relies heavily on local and regional allies for cover. Bin Laden has become an old revolutionary who refuses to retire though his time has passed.

While the tape's content appears to indicate that it was made recently, it has not yet been confirmed that it is an entirely new communication. From what STRATFOR has read of the statement so far, bin Laden does not even mention two of the incidents that have occurred to strengthen al Qaeda since his last message: the Nov. 26 attacks in Mumbai and militants' gains in northwest Pakistan. Some other strange omissions include the failure to mention U.S. President-elect Barack Obama by name (bin Laden refers only to "Bush's successor," although he does reportedly quote Vice President-elect Joe Biden directly) and the absence of the online advertising and hype that usually precede such a release from bin Laden.

The fact that bin Laden spent most of the message railing against the United States and Israel for the actions in Gaza does not mean that the tape is recent. Israel has constantly been involved in Gaza operations, and this subject has been one of bin Laden's main grievances on which he has spoken frequently. Compared to the message released Jan. 6 by Ayman al-Zawahiri (bin Laden's deputy), which commented specifically on Obama and on Egypt's failure to intervene in the Israeli strikes against Gaza, this message appears to go into much less detail.

Regardless of the content of bin Laden's message, the fact remains that the connection between these tapes and attacks carried out by al Qaeda prime is very weak. This is the seventh tape (counting both audio and video) bin Laden has made since 2007 with no significant attack to back it up. In recent years, al Qaeda prime has really posed a physical threat only to South Asia — an area of operations whose size hardly corresponds to al Qaeda prime's frequent calls for global jihad.

Without attacks to back it up, rhetoric appears to be bin Laden's sole remaining weapon. Meanwhile, other militant Islamist groups like Hamas and Hezbollah, and countries like Iran, are gaining much greater prestige as they confront their traditional enemies, like Israel, head-on. Without the street credibility of being a legitimate revolutionary threat, bin Laden and al Qaeda prime lose the ability to attract recruits and money — and bin Laden's appeal to supporters for both in his latest message is evidence of his declining stature.

Some of the omissions surrounding the tape also indicate al Qaeda prime's struggle to stay alive. If al Qaeda were healthy, a mention of the Mumbai attacks and the gains militants have made against the government in northwestern Pakistan would have been expected. However, al Qaeda prime's inability to capitalize on those gains shows just how much U.S. airstrikes have pinned the group down. The failure to advertise the message and hype its release indicates that al Qaeda prime faces a significant risk in getting an original tape from the source and distributing it online. Tipping off the United States that a tape would soon be released could compromise communication networks already worn thin by U.S. strikes in northwestern Pakistan.

Bin Laden (and other al Qaeda prime talking heads) will continue to make these tapes and, given that the al Qaeda leader has orchestrated successful attacks in the past, some will continue to listen to him. But without a major action to back up his threats, bin Laden's influence over the militant Islamist movement will fade. However, this does not mean the militant Islamist movement itself will fade. As the actions of groups like Hamas and Hezbollah (and Hezbollah's patron, Iran) show, plenty of people are prepared to become the world's top Islamist militant.

Taking Credit for Failure
Jan. 27, 2010

On Jan. 24, a voice purported to be that of Osama bin Laden claimed responsibility for the botched attempt to bring down Northwest Airlines Flight 253 on Christmas Day. The short one-minute and two-second audio statement, which was broadcast on Al Jazeera television, called the 23-year-old Nigerian suspect Umar Farouk Abdulmutallab a hero and threatened more attacks. The voice on the recording said the bombing attempt was in response to the situation in Gaza and that the United States can never dream of living in peace until Muslims have peace in the Palestinian territories. The speaker also said that attacks against the United States would continue as long as the United States continued to support Israel.

While the U.S. government has yet to confirm that the voice is that of bin Laden, Al Jazeera claims that the voice is indeed that of the al Qaeda leader. Bin Laden's health and welfare have been the topic of a lot of discussion and debate over the past several years, and many intelligence officials believe he is dead. Because of this, any time an audio recording purporting to be from bin Laden is released it receives heavy forensic scrutiny. Some technical experts believe that recent statements supposedly made by bin Laden have been cobbled together by manipulating portions of longer bin Laden messages that were previously recorded. It has been STRATFOR's position for several years that, whether bin Laden is dead or alive, the al Qaeda core has been marginalized by the efforts of the United States and its allies to the point where the group no longer poses a strategic threat.

Now, questions of bin Laden's status aside, the recording was most likely released through channels that helped assure Al Jazeera that the recording was authentic. This means that we can be somewhat confident that the message was released by the al Qaeda core. The fact that the al Qaeda core would attempt to take credit for a failed attack in a recording is quite interesting. But perhaps even more interesting is the core group's claim that the attack was conducted because of U.S. support for Israel and the treatment of the Palestinians living in Gaza.

Smoke and Mirrors

During the early years of al Qaeda's existence, the group did not take credit for attacks it conducted. In fact, it explicitly denied involvement. In interviews with the press, bin Laden often praised the attackers while, with a bit of a wink and a nod, he denied any connection to the attacks. Bin Laden issued public statements after the August 1998 East Africa embassy bombings and the 9/11 attacks flatly denying any involvement. In fact, bin Laden and al Qaeda continued to publicly deny any connection to the 9/11 attacks until after the U.S. invasion of Afghanistan. These denials of the 9/11 attacks have taken on a life of their own and have become the basis of conspiracy theories that the United States or Israel was behind the attacks (despite later statements by bin Laden and his deputy, Ayman al-Zawahiri, that contradicted earlier statements and claimed credit for 9/11).

In the years following 9/11, the al Qaeda core has continued to bask in the glory of that spectacularly successful attack, but it has not been able to produce the long-awaited encore. This is not for lack of effort; the al Qaeda core has been involved in several attempted attacks against the United States, such as the attempted shoe-bomb attack in December 2001, dispatching Jose Padilla to the United States in May of 2002 to purportedly try to conduct a dirty-bomb attack, and the August 2006 thwarted plot to attack trans-Atlantic airliners using liquid explosives. Interestingly, while each of these failed attempts has been tied to the al Qaeda core by intelligence and investigative efforts, the group did not publicly claim credit for any of them. While the group's leadership has made repeated threats that they were going to launch an attack that would dwarf 9/11, they simply have been unable to do so. Indeed, the only plot that could have come anywhere near the destruction of the 9/11 attacks was the liquid explosives plot, and that was foiled early on in the operational planning process — before the explosive devices were even fabricated.

Now, back to the failed bombing attempt on Christmas Day. First, the Yemeni franchise of al Qaeda, al Qaeda in the Arabian Peninsula (AQAP), has already claimed responsibility for the attack, and evidence strongly suggests that AQAP is the organization with which Abdulmutallab had direct contact. Indeed, while some members of AQAP have had prior contact with bin Laden, there is little to suggest that bin Laden himself or what remains of al Qaeda's core leadership has any direct role in planning any of the operations conducted by AQAP. The core group does not exercise that type of control over the activities of any of its regional groups. These groups are more like independent franchises that operate under the same brand name rather than parts of a single hierarchical organization. Each franchise has local leadership and is self-funding, and the franchises frequently diverge from global al Qaeda "corporate policies" in areas like target selection.

Furthermore, in an environment where the jihadists know that U.S. signals-intelligence efforts are keenly focused on the al Qaeda core and the regional franchise groups, discussing any type of operational information via telephone or e-mail from Yemen to Pakistan would be very dangerous — and terrible operational security. Using couriers would be more secure, but the al Qaeda core leadership is very cautious in its communications with the outside world (Hellfire missiles can have that effect on people), and any such communications will be very slow and deliberate. For the al Qaeda core leadership, the price of physical security has been the loss of operational control over the larger movement.

Taking things one step further, not only is the core of al Qaeda attempting to take credit for something it did not do, but it is claiming credit for an attack that did little more than severely burn the attacker in a very sensitive anatomical area. Some have argued that the attack was successful because it has instilled fear and caused the U.S. government to react, but clearly the attack would have had a far greater impact had the device detonated. The failed attack was certainly not what the operational planners had in mind when they dispatched Abdulmutallab on his mission.

This attempt by the al Qaeda core to pander for publicity, even though it means claiming credit for a botched attack, clearly demonstrates how far the core group has fallen since the days when bin Laden blithely denied responsibility for 9/11.

The Palestinian Focus

Since the beginning of bin Laden's public discourse, the Palestinian cause has been a consistent feature. His 1996 declaration of war and the 1998 fatwa declaring jihad against the West and Israel are prime examples. However, the reality of al Qaeda's activities has shown that, to bin Laden, the plight of the Palestinians has been less an area of genuine concern and more of a rhetorical device to exploit sympathy for the jihadist cause and draw Muslims to al Qaeda's banner.

Over the years, al Qaeda has worked very closely with a number of militant groups in a variety of places, including the Salafist Group for Preaching and Combat in Algeria, Jemaah Islamiyah in Indonesia and the East Turkestan Islamic Movement in China. However, while one of bin Laden's mentors, Abdullah Azzam, was a Palestinian, and there have been several Palestinians affiliated with al Qaeda over the years, the group has done little to support Palestinian resistance groups such as Hamas, even though Hamas (as the Palestinian offshoot of the Muslim Brotherhood) sprang from the same radical Egyptian Islamist milieu that produced al-Zawahiri's Egyptian Islamic Jihad (EIJ), which al-Zawahiri later folded into al Qaeda.

Jihadist militant groups such as Jund Ansar Allah have attempted to establish themselves in Gaza, but these groups were seen as problematic competition, rather than allies, and Hamas quickly stamped them out.

With little help coming from fellow Sunnis, Hamas has come to rely on Iran and Iran's Lebanese proxy, Hezbollah, as sources of funding, weapons and training. Even though this support is flowing across the Shiite-Sunni divide, actions speak louder than words, and Iran and Hezbollah have shown that they can deliver. In many ways, the political philosophy of Hamas (which has been sharply criticized by al-Zawahiri and other al Qaeda leaders) is far closer to that of Iran than to that of the jihadists. With Iran's help, Hamas has progressed from throwing rocks and firing homemade Qassam rockets to launching the longer range Grad and Fajr rockets and conducting increasingly effective irregular-warfare operations against the Israeli army.

Hezbollah's ability to eject Israel from southern Lebanon and its strong stand against the Israeli armed forces in the 2006 war made a strong impression in the Middle East. Iran, Hezbollah and Hamas are seen as very real threats to Israel, while al Qaeda has shown that it can produce a lot of anti-Israeli rhetoric but few results. Because of this, Iran and its proxies have become the vanguard of the fight against Israel, while al Qaeda is simply trying to keep its name in the press.

Claiming credit for failed attacks orchestrated by others and trying to latch on to the fight against Israel are just the latest signs that al Qaeda is trying almost too hard to remain relevant.

CHAPTER 4: JIHADISM
THE MOVEMENT

Net Assessment: An Extreme Ideology Unbound
Nov. 27, 2004

In the course of relatively few years, jihadism has burgeoned from a low-key movement seeking the ouster of corrupt regimes in the Muslim world into a global phenomenon that seeks to eradicate Western influence from that world. Though the movement is encapsulated in the minds of the public by the person of Osama bin Laden, it is important to understand that the phenomenon is not restricted to a particular group or brand of groups but rather is a broad ideological movement to which many disparate groups — separated by geography, individual motivations and even immediate political goals — may belong.

For our purposes, jihadism is defined as an ideology espoused by a fringe minority of various extremist Muslim groups, all operating on the periphery of the Islamist political spectrum. The movement has appropriated the notion of jihad ("righteous struggle") in calling for the use of force — against either military or civilian targets — by non-state actors whose ultimate objective is to establish an Islamic state.

The movement, which has been propelled by a number of events during the course of the past half-century, today is being driven forward chiefly by two factors: the continued decentralization of al Qaeda and the U.S. occupation of Iraq.

Origins of Jihadism

Jihadism is a subset of the overall Islamist movement — a larger, much more moderate movement which holds that Islam should form the political foundation for a state. According to this ideology, secular political institutions and regimes should be ousted in favor of state institutions that are governed by the dictates of the Koran. Theoretically and practically, Islamism would include both violent and non-violent actors; jihadism is the violent offshoot, which developed during the latter half of the 20th century.

Ideologically, the movement can be traced back to the first Arab-Israeli war, in 1948. During the 1970s, however, it gained momentum, with the emergence in Egypt of the Gamaah al-Islamiyah and Tandheem al Jihad — to be followed years later by numerous other groups throughout the Muslim world. Egypt's defeat in the 1967 Arab-Israeli war, coupled with Egyptian President Gamal Abdel Nasser's crackdown against the moderate Muslim Brotherhood, may have been the catalyst that pushed some already radical Muslims toward violent jihad. These events, together with the success of the Islamic revolution in Iran and the mujahideen victories against Soviet forces in Afghanistan, laid the foundation for the modern jihadist movement.

Palestinian scholar-turned-activist Abdallah Azzam, who played a leading role in recruiting Muslim volunteers to fight Soviet troops in Afghanistan during the 1980s, is seen as the godfather of the jihadist ideology. Azzam, who worked as a professor of Islamic jurisprudence in Saudi Arabia, initially was a member of the Muslim Brotherhood in Jordan and Egypt. His most famous written work is "Join the Caravan," published in the late 1980s, which has been an inspiration for many young Muslims.

Several other influential jihadists also hail from Egyptian groups: Sheikh Omar Abdel-Rehman, a blind activist-scholar, was the founder of Gamaah, and al Qaeda lieutenant Ayman al-Zawahiri emerged from the Tandheem al Jihad (Jihad Organization), which was involved in the 1981 assassination of Egyptian President Anwar el-Sadat. Among al-Zawahiri's works is a scathing attack on the moderate philosophy of the Muslim Brotherhood, titled Al Hasad al-Murr: al-Ikhwan al-Muslimoun fi Sittin Aman (The Bitter Harvest: The Muslim Brotherhood in Sixty Years). The movement also has been influenced by the thinking of Egyptian author Abdel-Salam al Faraj, whose most famous jihadist text is Faridah al Ghaibah (The Neglected Duty).

All of these men splintered off from the Brotherhood and grew intellectually closer to Wahhabism, a very strict interpretation of Islam. Eventually, in the mid-1990s, Wahhabis under the leadership of bin Laden seized control of the jihadist movement, which crystallized in the form of al Qaeda.

Prior to al Qaeda's emergence, the jihadist movement lacked a standard-bearer. Instead, it was a grouping of religious scholars and activists, rallying to various interpretations of the Koran and Sunnah. To some extent, that reality continues today — though the movement as a whole is heavily influenced by al Qaeda's Wahhabi extremism. However, al Qaeda does not represent the sum total of jihadism. Bin Laden views himself and his organization as a vanguard for the wider movement.

Ultimately, the jihadists are set apart from other Muslims by their use of jihad as a vehicle to establish an Islamic polity — a departure from the classic conception of jihad as an affair to be conducted by Islamic authorities, such as the caliphates and various local or regional emirates. The philosophy that non-state actors can appropriate jihad as a means to establishing an Islamic polity is an unprecedented intellectual development in the history of Islam.

The Decentralization Factor

Judging from recent statements attributed to both bin Laden and al-Zawahiri — and even to lesser al Qaeda lieutenants and acolytes,

such as the late Abdel Aziz al-Muqrin and Abu Musab al-Zarqawi —
it appears that al Qaeda is transforming itself from a strictly militant
group into a quasi-political organization, and simultaneously making
concerted efforts to disseminate its message at the grassroots level.

The political evolution is apparent in the most recent tape attributed to bin Laden, as well as in a publication he released in the aftermath of the March bombings in Madrid, announcing a 90-day truce
with European states. This transformation signals a practical approach
to the group's survival, given the global dragnet that has been under
way since the Sept. 11 attacks.

The evolution in al Qaeda's communications is more subtle, but
can be detected in a careful examination of the rhetoric used by senior
leaders.

For instance, in the last statement attributed to him, al-Zawahiri
called on all Muslims to increase their support for the jihadist movement. He encouraged all to take a lesson from the mujahideen in
Afghanistan and Chechnya and apply that lesson to their own lands
and lives. He also criticized those who restricted their support and
activities to the Israeli-Palestinian conflict, which has long been a
rhetorical pillar of the jihadist movement.

Also significant has been the emergence of more regional and
quasi-independent jihadist groups that act with little or no encour-
agement from al Qaeda "prime" — groups such as Jemaah Islamiyah
in Southeast Asia, the semi-independent al Qaeda cell active in
Saudi Arabia, and even al-Zarqawi's virtually independent Jamaat
al Tawheed wa al Jihad (Monotheism and Fighting Group) in Iraq,
which has renamed itself "Tandheem al Qaeda fi Bilad al Rafidain"
("Al Qaeda Organization in the Land of the Two Rivers").

All of these are Islamist militant groups with some sort of ties
to the al Qaeda hierarchy, and though the level of communication
maintained is debatable, the evidence that they are carrying on with
operations regardless is without question.

There is an important explanation for this self-motivation and
autonomy. Al Qaeda has always been a relatively small organization compared to the movement it sought to inspire. Sources have

told STRATFOR that many of the training camps al Qaeda ran in Afghanistan following the Soviet war served, importantly, as a kind of ideological exchange program — a way of exporting the jihadist philosophy to the four corners of the world. Whether the military training that supporters from various countries received ever was translated into militant action was insignificant; groups like al Qaeda rely on rhetorical and ideological support in much the same way that they rely on financial and logistical support. Any small-scale regional activity that can be linked back to al Qaeda only bolsters the image it seeks to create as a global entity representing the entire Muslim world.

In Iraq, al-Zarqawi is emerging as a perfect example of this trend. Though he was virtually unknown within the jihadist community before the Iraq war, al-Zarqawi now has nearly as much name recognition as bin Laden himself. His path from anonymity to media star is one to watch, particularly if it should be repeated in another theater of operations.

Al-Zarqawi, who trained at al Qaeda camps in Afghanistan, may or may not have had contact with bin Laden before being essentially cut loose by the organization years ago. He was involved in a variety of jihadist activities in Europe and an unrealized Y2K plot in Jordan before establishing himself — on the strength of several grisly beheading videos and other actions — as a potential rallying point for the global jihadist movement. Part of the explanation for his "success," despite his distance from al Qaeda prime, is the universal applicability of the jihadist message. Rhetorical calls to resist Western involvement and influence in Muslim lands and overthrow "corrupt" Muslim regimes are resounding throughout the Islamist world, perhaps more now than ever.

The U.S. Occupation

The U.S. invasion of Iraq has given new currency to jihadist calls for action. Despite widespread rhetoric condemning the plight of the Palestinians — even throughout the war in Afghanistan — the response of most Muslims to cries for jihad was one of inertia. Since the Sept. 11 attacks and U.S.-led and -inspired action against suspected terrorists in many parts of the globe, however, the perception that the West is at war with Islam itself has grown. Now, the presence of a bona fide military occupation force in a Muslim country, Iraq, is rousing the masses in ways that previous conflicts did not.

Prior to the U.S. invasion and occupation of Iraq, the rhetorical motivation for engaging in jihad was rather ephemeral. Much of the justification stemmed from U.S. support for Israel in the ongoing Palestinian conflict and the previous Arab-Israeli war. Essentially, the Palestinian struggle was branded as the struggle of all Muslims, and U.S. support for Israel was, by extension, portrayed as oppression of all Muslims.

The presence of U.S. military forces in Saudi Arabia also was cited as a justification — and unquestionably was a primary motivator for bin Laden personally — but this was received by most Muslims as something of a stretch. In their minds, it was more of a call to a primarily offensive operation against a potential future foe — a preemptive doctrine of jihad. This doctrine is unappealing to many, who believe that only the state can righteously conduct offensive jihad. Defensive jihad, by contrast, is the duty of every Muslim — and this is the view adopted of resisting U.S. forces in Iraq, similar to the struggles in Afghanistan, Chechnya and Bosnia.

Jihadist leaders also have pointed to the United States' enforcement of the U.N. embargo of Iraq and America's "cultural aggression" against Muslim lands, but these justifications pale in comparison with the invasion of Iraq, which incensed even many "moderate" Muslims. As a result, many now view the Sunni insurgents fighting Iraqi and coalition forces as legitimate mujahideen (religious fighters).

The U.S. military action also apparently has pushed many sympathizers of al Qaeda into taking action of their own. This appears to be the case in the seemingly random violence against Westerners in places like Saudi Arabia, where activists unaffiliated with al Qaeda (mostly youths) carry out targeted assassinations. Ultimately, the Iraq conflict could serve as the next forge in which future jihadists are molded — much as Afghanistan, Chechnya and the Balkans before.

That said, it is important to distinguish between Muslim support for anti-occupation struggles and al Qaeda-style terrorism. The former is a task-specific support — fighting what is perceived as a foreign occupation, as opposed to destabilizing legitimate governments in Muslim states. The majority of Muslims do not support the latter goal, and even in the context of Iraq, al-Zarqawi and other militants who engage in car-bombings, kidnappings and executions targeting non-combatants are frowned upon.

Meanwhile, many of the legal reforms and social changes, such as amendments to the curricula of the madrassas and promotion of more moderate forms of Islam, pushed forward by regimes in countries like Pakistan and Saudi Arabia — traditional bases of operations for al Qaeda — are being attributed directly to U.S. influence. In this way, jihadists are gaining some traction even from domestic, intra-Muslim issues in parts of the world where the United States has applied political or military pressure.

It is not clear how long this particular trend might continue, but for the time being the occupation of Iraq is providing a much-needed raison d'etre for the jihadist movement — and offers the potential for it to expand and survive.

Jihadism in 2009: The Trends Continue
Jan. 7, 2009

For the past several years, we have published an annual forecast for al Qaeda and the jihadist movement. Since the January 2006 forecast, we have focused heavily on the devolution of jihadism from a phenomenon focused primarily on al Qaeda the group to one based primarily on al Qaeda the movement. Last year, we argued that al Qaeda was struggling to remain relevant and that al Qaeda prime had been

STRATFOR'S 2008 FORECAST IN REVIEW:

WHAT WE GOT RIGHT:

- Al Qaeda core will focus on the ideological battle.
- Pakistan will be important as a potential flash point.
- The November 2007 addition of the Libyan Islamic Fighting Group (LIFG) to the global jihadist network will not pose a serious threat to the Libyan regime.
- Jihadists will kill more people with explosives and firearms than with chemical, biological or radiological weapons.

WHAT WE GOT MOSTLY RIGHT:

- The Algerian jihadist franchise, al Qaeda in the Islamic Maghreb (AQIM), will be hard-pressed in 2008, but not eliminated.
- Syria will use Fatah al-Islam as a destabilizing force in Lebanon.
- Jihadist operatives outside war zones will focus on soft targets.

WHAT WE MISSED:

- The jihadist franchises in Yemen resurged, and al Shabaab in Somalia found success.

marginalized in the physical battlefield. This marginalization of al Qaeda prime had caused that group to forfeit its position at the vanguard of the physical jihad, though it remained deeply involved in the leadership of the ideological battle.

As a quick reminder, STRATFOR views what most people refer to as "al Qaeda" as a global jihadist network rather than a monolithic entity. This network consists of three distinct entities. The first is a core vanguard, which we frequently refer to as al Qaeda prime, consisting of Osama bin Laden and his trusted associates. The second is composed of al Qaeda franchise groups such as al Qaeda in Iraq, and the third is the grassroots jihadist movement inspired by al Qaeda prime and the franchise groups.

As indicated by the title of this forecast, we believe that the trends we have discussed in previous years will continue and that al Qaeda prime has become marginalized on the physical battlefield (to the extent that we have not even included their name in the title of this assessment). The regional jihadist franchises and grassroots operatives pose a much more significant threat in terms of security concerns, though it is important to note that those concerns will remain tactical and not rise to the level of a strategic threat. In our view, the sort of strategic challenge that al Qaeda prime posed with the 9/11 attacks simply cannot be replicated without a major change in geopolitical alignments — a change we do not anticipate in 2009.

2008 in Review

Before diving into our forecast for the coming year, let's take a quick look back at what we said would happen in 2008 and see what we got right and what we did not.

What we got right:

- Al Qaeda core focused on the ideological battle. Another year has passed without a physical attack by the al Qaeda core. As we noted last October, al Qaeda spent a tremendous amount of effort in 2008 fighting the ideological battle. The core leadership still appears to be very intent on countering the thoughts presented in a book written in 2007 by Sayyed Imam al-Sharif, also known as Dr. Fadl, an imprisoned Egyptian radical and a founder (with Ayman al-Zawahiri) of Egyptian Islamic Jihad. Al-Sharif's book is seen as such a threat because he provides theological arguments that counter many of the core teachings used by al Qaeda to justify jihadism. On Dec. 13, an 85-page treatise by one of al Qaeda's leading religious authorities,

Abu-Yahya al-Libi, was released to jihadist Web sites in the latest of al Qaeda's many efforts to counter Dr. Fadl's arguments.

- Pakistan will be important as a potential flashpoint. Eight days after we wrote this, former Pakistani Prime Minister Benazir Bhutto was assassinated. Since then, Pakistan has become the focal point on the physical battlefield.

- The November 2007 addition of the Libyan Islamic Fighting Group (LIFG) to the global jihadist network will not pose a serious threat to the Libyan regime. The Libyans have deftly used a combination of carrots and sticks to divide and control the LIFG.

- Jihadists will kill more people with explosives and firearms than with chemical, biological or radiological weapons. We saw no jihadist attacks using WMD in 2008.

What we got mostly right:

- The Algerian jihadist franchise, al Qaeda in the Islamic Maghreb (AQIM), will be hard-pressed in 2008, but not eliminated. AQIM succeeded in launching a large number of attacks in the first eight months of 2008, killing as many people as it did in all of 2007. But since then, the Algerian government has been making progress, and the jihadist group has conducted only two attacks since August 2008. The Algerians also are working closely with neighboring countries to combat AQIM, and the group is definitely feeling the heat. On Dec. 23, 2008, the Algerian government reportedly rejected a truce offered by AQIM leader Yahia Djouadi. Djouadi offered that al Qaeda would cease attacks on foreigners operating in oil fields in Algeria and Mauritania if the Algerian security service would cease targeting al Qaeda members in the Sahel region. The group is still alive, and government pressure appears to have affected its operational ability in recent months, but it did

158

take a bit longer than we anticipated for the pressure to make a difference.

- Syria will use Fatah al-Islam as a destabilizing force in Lebanon. We had intelligence last year suggesting that the Syrians were going to press the use of their jihadist proxies in Lebanon — specifically Fatah al-Islam. We saw a bit of this type of activity in late May, but not as much as anticipated. By November, Syria actually decided to cut ties with Fatah al-Islam.
- Jihadist operatives outside war zones will focus on soft targets. Major terrorist strikes in Islamabad and New Delhi were conducted against hotels, soft targets STRATFOR has talked about being particularly vulnerable for many years now. Other attacks in India focused on markets and other public places. While most of the attacks against hard targets came in war zones like Iraq and Afghanistan, there were a few attacks against hard targets in places like Pakistan, Yemen and Turkey. Granted, the Sanaa and Istanbul attacks were unsuccessful, but they were attacks against hard targets nonetheless.

What we missed:

- The jihadist franchises in Yemen resurged and al Shabaab in Somalia found success. While we quickly picked up on these trends in April and May respectively (and beat most others to the punch with some very good analysis on these topics), we clearly did not predict them in December 2007. We knew that the influx of fighters from Iraq was going to impact countries in the region, but we didn't specifically focus on Yemen and Somalia.

The Year Ahead

We anticipate that we will see the United States continue its campaign of decapitation strikes against al Qaeda leadership. While this campaign has not managed to get bin Laden or al-Zawahiri, it has proved quite successful at causing the al Qaeda apex leadership to lie low and become marginalized from the physical jihad. The campaign also has killed a long list of key al Qaeda operational commanders and trainers. As noted above, we believe the core leadership is very concerned about the ideological battle being waged against it — the only real way the theology of jihadism can be defeated — and will continue to focus their efforts on that battlespace.

As long as the ideology of jihadism survives (it has been around since the late 1980s), the jihadists' war against the world will continue, oscillating between periods of high and low intensity. In the coming year, we believe the bulk of physical attacks will continue to be conducted by regional jihadist franchise groups and to a lesser extent by grassroots jihadists.

With the lack of regional franchises in North America, we do not see a strategic threat to the United States. However, as seen by the recent convictions in the Fort Dix plot trial, or even in the late October case where a U.S. citizen apparently committed a suicide bombing on behalf of al Shabaab in Somalia, the threat of simple attacks against soft targets in the United States remains. We were again surprised that no jihadist attacks occurred in the United States in 2008. Given the vulnerabilities that exist in an open society and the ease of attack, we cannot rule out an attack in 2009.

In Europe, where AQIM and other jihadist franchises have a greater presence and infrastructure, there is a greater threat that these franchises will commit sophisticated attacks. It must be recognized, though, that they will have a far harder time acquiring weapons and explosives to conduct such attacks in the United Kingdom or France than they would in Algeria or Pakistan. Because of this, we anticipate that they will continue to focus on soft targets in Europe. Due to differences between the Muslim communities in the United States and Europe, the grassroots operatives have been more active in Europe than they are in the United States. The May 22, 2008, attempted bombing at the Giraffe Cafe by a Muslim convert in Exeter serves as a good reminder of this.

Jihadist Franchises

After failing last year to predict the resurgence of the jihadist franchises in Yemen and Somalia, we will be keeping a sharp eye on both for 2009. Somalia continues to be a basket case of a country, and the instability there is providing an opportunity for al Shabaab to flourish. There is currently an attempt under way to bring stability to Somalia, but we anticipate that it will not succeed, due to the militant factionalism in the country. The only thing working against al Shabaab and their jihadist brethren is that the Somali jihadists appear to be as fractious as the rest of the country; al Shabaab is itself a splinter of the Supreme Islamic Courts Council (SICC), which ruled Somalia briefly before the Ethiopian invasion in 2006. There are currently as many as four different jihadist factions fighting one another for control over various areas of Somalia — in addition to fighting foreign troops and the interim government.

In Yemen, things have been eerily quiet since the Sept. 17 attack against the U.S. Embassy in Sanaa and the government campaign to go after the group behind that attack. Six gunmen were killed in the attack itself, and the Yemenis have arrested numerous others whom they claim were involved in planning the attack. The Yemenis also killed or captured several significant jihadists prior to the September attack. But given the large number of Yemenis involved in the fighting in Iraq, the number of Saudi militants who have traveled to Yemen due to pressure at home, and the Salafist-jihadist influence within Yemen's security and intelligence apparatus, it will be possible for the two jihadist franchises in Yemen to recover if the Yemenis give them breathing space.

Meanwhile, though Iraq is far calmer than it was a few years back, a resurgence in jihadist activity is possible. One of the keys to calming down the many jihadist groups in Iraq was the formation of the Awakening Councils, which are made up of many Sunni and former Baathist (and some former jihadist) militants placed on the U.S. payroll. With the changes in Iraq, responsibility for these Awakening Councils has been passed to the Iraqi government. If the

Shiite-dominated government decides not to pay the councils, many of the militants-turned-security officers might return to their old ways — especially if the pay from jihadist groups is right. Intelligence reports indicate that Baghdad plans to pay only a fraction of the approximately 100,000 men currently serving in the Awakening Councils. The Iraqi central government apparently plans to offer the bulk of them civilian jobs or job training, but we are skeptical that this will work.

Elsewhere, Pakistan is once again the critical location for the jihadists. Not only is Pakistan the home of the al Qaeda core leadership as its pursues its ideological war, it also is home to a number of jihadist groups, from the Afghan Taliban and the Tehrik-i-Taliban Pakistan in the northwest to Lashkar-e-Taiba and Jaish-e-Mohammed in the northeast, among several others. The coming year might prove to be pivotal in global efforts against the jihadists in Pakistan. Pakistan already is a country in crisis, and in some ways, it is hard to imagine it getting much worse. But if Pakistan continues to destabilize, it could very well turn into a failed country (albeit a failed country with a nuclear arsenal). Before Pakistan becomes a failed state, there are a number of precursor stages it probably will pass through. The most immediate stage would entail the fall of most of the North-West Frontier Province to the jihadists, something that could happen this year.

This type of anarchy in Pakistan could give the jihadists an opportunity to exert control in a way similar to what they have done in places like Afghanistan and Somalia (and already in the Pakistani badlands along the Afghan border). If, on the other hand, Pakistan is somehow able to hold on, re-establish control over its territory and its rogue intelligence agency and begin to cooperate with the United States and other countries fighting the jihadists, such a development could deal a terrible blow to the aspirations of the jihadists on both the physical and ideological battlefields. Given the number of plots linked to Pakistan in recent years, including the Nov. 26 Mumbai attack and almost every significant plot since 9/11, all eyes will be watching Pakistan carefully.

The Jihadists' Strategic Dilemma
Dec. 7, 2009

With U.S. President Barack Obama's announcement of his strategy in Afghanistan, the U.S.-jihadist war has entered a new phase. With its allies, the United States has decided to increase its focus on the Afghan war while continuing to withdraw from Iraq. Along with focusing on Afghanistan, it follows that there will be increased Western attention on Pakistan. Meanwhile, the question of what to do with Iran remains open and is, in turn, linked to U.S.-Israeli relations. The region from the Mediterranean to the Hindu Kush remains in a war or near-war status. In a fundamental sense, U.S. strategy has not shifted under Obama: The United States remains in a spoiling-attack state.

As we have discussed, the primary U.S. interest in this region is twofold. The first aspect is to prevent the organization of further major terrorist attacks on the United States. The second is to prevent al Qaeda and other radical Islamist groups from taking control of any significant countries.

U.S. operations in this region consist mainly of spoiling attacks aimed at frustrating the jihadists' plans rather than at imposing Washington's will in the region. The United States lacks the resources to impose its will and ultimately doesn't need to. Rather, it needs to wreck its adversaries' plans. In both Afghanistan and Iraq, the primary American approach consists of this tack. That is the nature of spoiling attacks. Obama has thus continued the Bush administration's approach to the war, though he has shifted some details.

The Jihadist Viewpoint

It is therefore time to consider the war from the jihadist point of view. This is a difficult task given that the jihadists do not constitute a single, organized force with a command structure and staff that could express that view. It is compounded by the fact that al Qaeda prime, our term for the original al Qaeda that ordered and organized the attacks on 9/11 and in Madrid and London, is now largely shattered. While bearing this in mind, it must be remembered that this fragmentation is both a strategic necessity and a weapon of war for jihadists. The United States can strike the center of gravity of any jihadist force. It naturally cannot strike what doesn't exist, so the jihadist movement has been organized to deny the United States that center of gravity, or command structure that, if destroyed, would leave the movement wrecked. Thus, even were Osama bin Laden killed or captured, the jihadist movement is set up to continue.

So although we cannot speak of a jihadist viewpoint in the sense that we can speak of an American viewpoint, we can ask these questions: If we were a jihadist fighter at the end of 2009, what would the world look like to us, what would we want to achieve and what might we do to try to achieve that?

We must bear in mind that al Qaeda began the war with a core strategic intent, namely, to spark revolutions in the Sunni Muslim world by overthrowing existing regimes and replacing them with jihadist regimes. This was part of the jihadist group's long-term strategy to recreate a multinational Islamist empire united under al Qaeda's interpretation of Shariah.

The means toward this end involved demonstrating to the Muslim masses that their regimes were complicit with the leading Christian power, i.e., the United States, and that only American backing kept these Sunni regimes in power. By striking the United States on Sept. 11, al Qaeda wanted to demonstrate that the United States was far more vulnerable than believed, by extension demonstrating that U.S. client regimes were not as powerful as they appeared. This was meant to give the Islamic masses a sense that uprisings against Muslim regimes not dedicated to Shariah could succeed. In their view, any American military response — an inevitability after 9/11 — would further incite the Muslim masses rather than intimidate them.

The last eight years of war have ultimately been disappointing to the jihadists, however. Rather than a massive uprising in the Muslim world, not a single regime has been replaced with a jihadist regime.

The primary reason has been that Muslim regimes allied with the United States decided they had more to fear from the jihadists than from the Americans, and chose to use their intelligence and political power to attack and suppress the jihadists. In other words, rather than trigger an uprising, the jihadists generated a strengthened anti-jihadist response from existing Muslim states. The spoiling attacks in Afghanistan and Iraq, as well as in other countries in the Horn of Africa and North Africa, generated some support for the jihadists, but that support has since diminished and the spoiling attacks have disrupted these countries sufficiently to make them unsuitable as bases of operation for anything more than local attacks. In other words, the attacks tied the jihadists up in local conflicts, diverting them from operations against the United States and Europe.

Under this intense pressure, the jihadist movement has fragmented, though it continues to exist. Incapable of decisive action at the moment, it has goals beyond surviving as a fragmented entity, albeit with some fairly substantial fragments. And it is caught on the horns of a strategic dilemma.

Operationally, jihadists continue to be engaged against the United States. In Afghanistan, the jihadist movement is relying on the Taliban to tie down and weaken American forces. In Iraq, the remnants of the jihadist movement are doing what they can to shatter the U.S.-sponsored coalition government in Baghdad and further tie down American forces by attacking Shiites and key members of the Sunni community. Outside these two theaters, the jihadists are working to attack existing Muslim governments collaborating with the United States — particularly Pakistan — but with periodic attacks striking other Muslim states.

These attacks represent the fragmentation of the jihadists. Their ability to project power is limited. By default, they have accordingly adopted a strategy of localism, in which their primary intent is to strike existing governments while simultaneously tying down American forces in a hopeless attempt to stabilize the situation.

The strategic dilemma is this: The United States is engaged in a spoiling action with the primary aim of creating conditions in which jihadists are bottled up fighting indigenous forces rather than being free to plan attacks on the United States or systematically try to pull down existing regimes. And the current jihadist strategy plays directly into American hands. First, the attacks cause Muslim regimes to deploy their intelligence and security forces against the jihadists, which is precisely what the United States wants. Second, the strategy shifts jihadist strength away from transnational actions to local actions, which is also what the United States wants. These local attacks, which kill mostly Muslims, also serve to alienate many Muslims from the jihadists.

The jihadists are currently playing directly into U.S. hands because, rhetoric aside, the United States cannot regard instability in the Islamic world as a problem. Let's be more precise on this: An ideal outcome for the United States would be the creation of stable, pro-American regimes in the region eager and able to attack and destroy jihadist networks. There are some regimes in the region like this, such as Saudi Arabia and Egypt. The probability of creating such stable, eager and capable regimes in places like Iraq or Afghanistan is unlikely in the extreme. The second-best outcome for the United States involves a conflict in which the primary forces battling — and neutralizing — each other are Muslim, with the American forces in a secondary role. This has been achieved to some extent in Iraq. Obama's goal is to create a situation in Afghanistan in which Afghan government forces engage Taliban forces with little or no U.S. involvement. Meanwhile, in Pakistan the Americans would like to see an effective effort by Islamabad to suppress jihadists throughout Pakistan. If they cannot get suppression, the United States will settle for a long internal conflict that would tie down the jihadists.

A Self-Defeating Strategy

The jihadists are engaged in a self-defeating strategy when they spread out and act locally. The one goal they must have, and the one outcome the United States fears, is the creation of stable jihadist regimes. The strategy of locally focused terrorism has proved ineffective. It not only fails to mobilize the Islamic masses, it also creates substantial coalitions seeking to suppress the jihadists.

The jihadist attack on the United States has failed. The presence of U.S. forces in Iraq and Afghanistan has reshaped the behavior of regional governments. Fear of instability generated by the war has generated counteractions by regional governments. Contrary to what the jihadists expected or hoped for, there was no mass uprising and therefore no counter to anti-jihadist actions by regimes seeking to placate the United States. The original fear, that the U.S. presence in Iraq and Afghanistan would generate massive hostility, was not wrong. But the hostility did not strengthen the jihadists, and instead generated anti-jihadist actions by governments.

From the jihadist point of view, it would seem essential to get the U.S. military out of the region and to relax anti-jihadist actions by regional security forces. Continued sporadic and ineffective action by jihadists achieves nothing and generates forces with which they can't cope. If the United States withdrew, and existing tensions within countries like Egypt, Saudi Arabia or Pakistan were allowed to mature undisturbed, new opportunities might present themselves.

Most significantly, the withdrawal of U.S. troops would strengthen Iran. The jihadists are no friends of Shiite Iran, and neither are Iran's neighbors. In looking for a tool for political mobilization in the Gulf region or in Afghanistan absent a U.S. presence, the Iranian threat would best serve the jihadists. The Iranian threat combined with the weakness of regional Muslim powers would allow the jihadists to join a religious and nationalist opposition to Tehran. The ability to join religion and nationalism would turn the local focus from something that takes the jihadists away from regime change to something that might take them toward it.

The single most powerful motivator for an American withdrawal would be a period of open quiescence. An openly stated consensus for standing down, in particular because of a diminished terrorist threat, would facilitate something the Obama administration wants most of all: a U.S. withdrawal from the region. Providing the Americans with a justification for leaving would open the door for new possibilities.

The jihadists played a hand on 9/11 that they hoped would be a full house. It turned into a bust. When that happens, you fold your hand and play a new one. And there is always a hand being dealt so long as you have some chips left.

The challenge here is that the jihadists have created a situation in which they have defined their own credibility in terms of their ability to carry out terrorist attacks, however poorly executed or counterproductive they have become. Al Qaeda prime's endless calls for action have become the strategic foundation for the jihadists: Action has become an end in itself. The manner in which the jihadists have survived as a series of barely connected pods of individuals scattered across continents has denied the United States a center of gravity to strike. It has also turned the jihadists from a semi-organized force into one incapable of defining strategic shifts.

The jihadists' strategic dilemma is that they have lost the 2001–2008 phase of the war but are not defeated. To begin to recoup, they must shift their strategy. But they lack the means for doing so because of what they have had to do to survive. At the same time, there are other processes in play. The Taliban, which have even more reason to want the United States out of Afghanistan, might shift to an antijihadist strategy: They could liquidate al Qaeda, return to power in Afghanistan and then reconsider their strategy later. So, too, in other areas.

From the U.S. point of view, an open retreat by the jihadists would provide short-term relief but long-term problems. The moment when the enemy sues for peace is the moment when the pressure should be increased rather than decreased. But direct U.S. interests in the region are so minimal that a more distant terrorist threat will be handled in a more distant future. Since the jihadists are too fragmented to take strategic positions, U.S. pressure will continue in any event.

Oddly enough, as much as the United States is uncomfortable in the position it is in, the jihadists are in a much worse position.

Jihadism in 2010: A Transnational Franchise
Jan. 6, 2010

For the past several years, STRATFOR has published an annual forecast on al Qaeda and the jihadist movement. Since our first jihadist forecast in January 2006, we have focused heavily on the devolution of jihadism from a phenomenon primarily involving the core al Qaeda group to one based mainly on the wider jihadist movement and the devolving, decentralized threat it poses.

The central theme of last year's forecast was that al Qaeda was an important force on the ideological battlefield, but that the efforts of the United States and its allies had marginalized the group on the physical battlefield and kept it bottled up in a limited geographic area. Because of this, we forecast that the most significant threat in terms of physical attacks stemmed from regional jihadist franchises and grassroots operatives and not the al Qaeda core. We also wrote that we believed the threat posed by such attacks would remain tactical and not rise to the level of a strategic threat. To reflect this reality, we even dropped al Qaeda from the title of our annual forecast and simply named it Jihadism in 2009: The Trends Continue.

The past year proved to be very busy in terms of attacks and thwarted plots emanating from jihadist actors. But, as forecast, the primary militants involved in carrying out these terrorist plots were almost exclusively from regional jihadist groups and grassroots operatives, and not militants dispatched by the al Qaeda core. We anticipate that this dynamic will continue, and, if anything, the trend will be for some regional franchise groups to become even more involved in transnational attacks, thus further usurping the position of al Qaeda prime at the vanguard of jihadism on the physical battlefield.

A Note on 'Al Qaeda'

As a quick reminder, STRATFOR views what most people refer to as "al Qaeda" as a global jihadist network rather than a monolithic entity. This network consists of three distinct entities. The first is a core vanguard organization, which we frequently refer to as al Qaeda prime or the al Qaeda core. The al Qaeda core is comprised of Osama bin Laden and his small circle of close, trusted associates, such as Ayman al-Zawahiri. Due to intense pressure by the U.S. government and its allies, this core group has been reduced in size since 9/11 and remains relatively small because of operational security concerns. This insular group is laying low in Pakistan near the Afghan border and comprises only a small portion of the larger jihadist universe.

The second layer of the network is composed of local or regional terrorist or insurgent groups that have adopted jihadist ideology. Some of these groups have publicly claimed allegiance to bin Laden and the al Qaeda core and become what we refer to as franchise groups, like al Qaeda in the Islamic Maghreb (AQIM) or al Qaeda in the Arabian Peninsula (AQAP). Other groups may adopt some or all of al Qaeda's jihadist ideology and cooperate with the core group, but they will maintain their independence for a variety of reasons. Such groups include the Tehrik-i-Taliban Pakistan (TTP), Lashkar-e-Taiba (LeT) and Harkat-ul-Jihad e-Islami (HUJI). Indeed, in the case of some larger organizations such as LeT, some of the group's factions may actually oppose close cooperation with al Qaeda.

The third and broadest layer of the network is the grassroots jihadist movement, that is, people inspired by the al Qaeda core and the franchise groups but who may have little or no actual connection to these groups.

As we move down this hierarchy, we also move down in operational capability and expertise in what we call terrorist tradecraft — the set of skills required to conduct a terrorist attack. The operatives belonging to the al Qaeda core are generally better trained than their regional counterparts, and both of these layers tend to be far better trained than the grassroots operatives. Indeed, many grassroots operatives travel to places like Pakistan and Yemen in order to seek training from these other groups.

The Internet has long proved to be an important tool for these groups to reach out to potential grassroots operatives. Jihadist chat rooms and Web sites provide indoctrination in jihadist ideology and also serve as a means for aspiring jihadists to make contact with like-minded individuals and even the jihadist groups themselves.

2009 Forecast Review

Overall, our 2009 forecast was fairly accurate. As noted above, we wrote that the United States would continue its operations to decapitate the al Qaeda core and that this would cause the group to be marginalized from the physical jihad, and that has happened.

While we missed forecasting the resurgence of jihadist militant groups in Yemen and Somalia in 2008, in our 2009 forecast we covered these two countries carefully. We wrote that the al Qaeda franchises in Yemen had taken a hit in 2008 but that they could recover in 2009 given the opportunity. Indeed, the groups received a significant boost when they merged into a single group that also incorporated the remnants of al Qaeda in Saudi Arabia, which had been forced by Saudi security to flee the country. We closely followed this new group, which named itself al Qaeda in the Arabian Peninsula (AQAP), and STRATFOR was the first organization we know of to discuss the threat AQAP posed to civil aviation when we raised this subject on Sept. 2 and elaborated on it Sept. 16, in an analysis titled "Convergence: The Challenge of Aviation Security." That threat manifested itself in the attempt to destroy an airliner traveling from Amsterdam to Detroit on Christmas Day 2009 — an operation that very nearly succeeded.

Regarding Somalia, we have also been closely following al Shabaab and the other jihadist groups there, such as Hizbul Islam. Al Shabaab publicly pledged allegiance to Osama bin Laden in September 2009 and therefore has formally joined the ranks of al Qaeda's regional franchise groups. However, as we forecast last January, while the instability present in Somalia provides al Shabaab the opportunity to flourish, the factionalization of the country (including the jihadist groups operating there) has also served to keep al Shabaab from dominating the other actors and assuming control of the country.

We also forecast that, while Iraq had been relatively quiet in 2008, the level of violence there could surge in 2009 due to the Awakening Councils being taken off the U.S. payroll and having their control transferred to the Shiite-dominated Iraqi government, which might not pay them and integrate them into the armed forces. Indeed, since August, we have seen three waves of major coordinated attacks against Iraqi ministry buildings in Baghdad linked to the al Qaeda affiliate in Iraq, the Islamic State of Iraq. Since this violence is tied to the political situation in Iraq, and there is a clear correlation between the funds being cut to the Awakening Councils and these attacks, we anticipate that this violence will continue through the parliamentary elections in March. The attacks could even continue after that, if the Sunni powers in Iraq deem that their interests are not being addressed appropriately.

As in 2008, we paid close attention in 2009 to the situation in Pakistan. This not only was because Pakistan is the home of the al Qaeda core's leadership but also because of the threat that the TTP and the other jihadist groups in the country posed to the stability of the nuclear-armed state. As we watched Pakistan for signs that it was becoming a failed state, we noted that the government was actually making considerable headway in its fight against its jihadist insurgency. Indeed, by late in the year, the Pakistanis had launched not only a successful offensive in Swat and the adjacent districts but also an offensive into South Waziristan, the heart of the TTP's territory.

We also forecast that the bulk of the attacks worldwide in 2009 would be conducted by regional jihadist franchise groups and, to a lesser extent, grassroots jihadists, rather than the al Qaeda core, which was correct.

In relation to attacks against the United States, we wrote that we did not see a strategic threat to the United States from the jihadists, but that the threat of simple attacks against soft targets remained in 2009. We said we had been surprised that there were no such attacks in 2008 but that, given the vulnerabilities that existed and the ease with which such attacks could be conducted, we believed they were certainly possible. During 2009, we did see simple attacks by grassroots operatives in Little Rock, Arkansas, and at Fort Hood, Texas, along with several other grassroots plots thwarted by authorities.

Forecast for 2010

In the coming year we believe that, globally, we will see many of the trends continue from last year. We believe that the al Qaeda core will continue to be marginalized on the physical battlefield and struggle to remain relevant on the ideological battlefield. The regional jihadist franchise groups will continue to be at the vanguard of the physical battle, and the grassroots operatives will remain a persistent, though lower-level, threat.

One thing we noticed in recent months was that the regional groups were becoming more transnational in their attacks, with AQAP involved in the attack on Saudi Deputy Interior Minister Prince Mohammed bin Nayef in Saudi Arabia as well as the trans-Atlantic airliner-bombing plot on Christmas Day. Additionally, we saw HUJI planning an attack against the Jyllands-Posten newspaper and cartoonist Kurt Westergaard in Denmark, and on Jan. 1, 2010, a Somali man reportedly associated with al Shabaab broke into Westergaard's home armed with an axe and knife and allegedly tried to kill him. We believe that in 2010 we will see more examples of regional groups like al Shabaab and AQAP reaching out to become more transnational, perhaps even conducting attacks in the United States and Europe.

We also believe that, due to the open nature of the U.S. and European societies and the ease of conducting attacks against them, we will see more grassroots plots, if not successful attacks, in the United States and Europe in the coming year. The concept behind AQAP leader Nasir al-Wahayshi's article calling for jihadists to conduct simple attacks against a variety of targets may be gaining popularity among grassroots jihadists. Certainly, the above-mentioned attack in Denmark involving an axe and knife was simple in nature. It could also have been deadly had the cartoonist not had a panic room within his residence. We will be watching for more simple attacks.

As far as targets, we believe that they will remain largely the same for 2010. Soft targets such as hotels will continue to be popular, since most jihadists lack the ability to attack hard targets outside of conflict zones. However, jihadists have demonstrated a continuing fixation on attacking commercial aviation targets, and we can anticipate additional plots and attacks focusing on aircraft.

Regionally, we will be watching for the following:

- Pakistan: Can the United States find and kill the al Qaeda core's leadership? A Pakistani official told the Chinese Xinhua news agency on Jan. 4 that terrorism will come to an end in Pakistan in 2010, but we are not nearly so optimistic. Even though the military has made good progress in its South Waziristan offensive, most of the militants moved to other areas of Pakistan rather than engage in frontal combat with Pakistan's army. The area along the border with Pakistan is rugged and has proved hard to pacify for hundreds of years. We don't think the Pakistanis will be able to bring the area under control in only one year. Clearly, the Pakistanis have made progress, but they are not out of the woods. The TTP has launched a number of attacks in the Punjabi core of Pakistan (and in Karachi) and we see no end to this violence in 2010.

- Afghanistan: We will continue to closely monitor jihadist actors in this war-torn country. Our forecast for this conflict is included in our Annual Forecast 2010, published on Jan. 4.

- Yemen: We will be watching closely to see if AQAP will follow the normal jihadist group lifespan of making a big splash, coming to the notice of the world and then being hit heavily by the host government with U.S. support. This pattern was exhibited a few years back by AQAP's Saudi al Qaeda brethren, and judging by the operations in Yemen over the past month, it looks like 2010 might be a tough year for the group. It is important to note that the strikes against the group on Dec. 17 and Dec. 24 predated the Christmas bombing attempt, and the pressure on them will undoubtedly be ratcheted up considerably in the wake of that attack. Even as the memory of the Christmas Day attack begins to fade in the media and political circles, the focus on Yemen will continue in the counterterrorism community.

- Indonesia: Can Tanzim Qaedat al-Jihad find an effective leader to guide it back from the edge of destruction after the death of Noordin Mohammad Top and the deaths or captures of several of his top lieutenants? Or will the Indonesians be able to enjoy further success against the group's surviving members?

- North Africa: Will AQIM continue to shy away from the al Qaeda core's targeting philosophy and essentially function as the Salafist Group for Preaching and Combat with a different name in Algeria? Or will AQIM shift back toward al Qaeda's philosophy of attacking the far enemy and using suicide bombers and large vehicle bombs? In Mauritania, Niger and Mali, will the AQIM-affiliated cells there be able to progress beyond amateurish attacks and petty banditry to become a credible militant organization?

- Somalia: We believe the factionalism in Somalia and within the jihadist community there will continue to hamper al Shabaab. The questions we will be looking to answer are: Will al Shabaab be able to gain significant control of areas of the country that can be used to harbor and train foreign militants? And, will the group decide to use its contacts within the Somali diaspora to conduct attacks in East Africa, South Africa, Australia, Europe and the United States? We believe that al Shabaab is on its way to becoming a transnational player and that 2010 may well be the year that it breaks out and then draws international attention like AQAP has done in recent months.

- India: We anticipate that Kashmiri jihadist groups will continue to plan attacks against India in an effort to stir-up communal violence in that country and stoke tensions between

175

India and Pakistan — and provide a breather to the jihadist groups being pressured by the government of Pakistan.

As long as the ideology of jihadism survives, the jihadists will be able to recruit new militants and their war against the world will continue. The battle will oscillate between periods of high and low intensity as regional groups rise in power and are taken down. We don't believe jihadists pose a strategic geopolitical threat on a global, or even regional, scale, but they will certainly continue to launch attacks and kill people in 2010.

The Grassroots Paradox
March 18, 2010

Last week, rumors that Adam Gadahn had been arrested in Karachi, Pakistan, quickly swept through the global media. When the dust settled, it turned out that the rumors were incorrect; the person arrested was not the American-born al Qaeda spokesman. The excitement generated by the rumors overshadowed a message from Gadahn that the al Qaeda media arm As-Sahab had released on March 7, the same day as the reported arrest. While many of the messages from al Qaeda figures that As-Sahab has released over the past several years have been repetitive and quite unremarkable, after watching Gadahn's March 7 message, we believe that it is a message too interesting to ignore.

The Message

In the message, which was titled "A Call to Arms," Gadahn starts by telling jihadists to strike targets that are close to them. He repeats the al Qaeda doctrinal position that jihad is a personal, religiously mandated duty for every able-bodied Muslim. He then tells his audience that "it is for you, like your heroic Mujahid brother Nidal Hasan, to decide how, when and where you discharge this duty. But whatever you do, don't wait for tomorrow to do what can be done today, and don't wait for others to do what you can do yourself."

As the message progresses, Gadahn's praise of Fort Hood shooter Hasan continues. Gadahn lifts up Hasan as an example for other Muslims to emulate: "The Mujahid brother Nidal Hasan is a pioneer, a trailblazer and a role-model who has opened a door, lit a path and shown the way forward for every Muslim who finds himself among the unbelievers and yearns to discharge his duty to Allah." He adds that Hasan was the "ideal role model" for Muslims serving in the armed forces of Western countries and of their Muslim allies. Gadahn's message is clearly intended to encourage more jihadists to emulate Hasan and conduct lone-wolf terrorist attacks.

Regarding the planning of such attacks, Gadahn praises Hasan for being a careful planner and for not engaging in a hasty, reckless or poorly planned operation. He states that Hasan clearly learned from the mistakes of others and did not repeat them. Although Gadahn does not specify particular plots in which he believes mistakes were made by grassroots jihadists, he is undoubtedly referring to cases such as the May 2009 arrest of a group of grassroots jihadists in White Plains, N.Y., who came to the attention of authorities when they sought help from a man who turned out to be an FBI informant. Gadahn praises Hasan for practicing careful operational security by keeping his plans to himself and for not discussing them over the phone or Internet. He also notes that Hasan did not make the mistake of confiding in a person who might have been an FBI informant, as several other plotters have done. Gadahn also says Hasan "didn't unnecessarily raise his security profile or waste money better spent on the operation itself by traveling abroad to acquire skills and instructions which could easily be acquired at home, or indeed, deduced by using one's own powers of logic and reasoning."

When discussing methods lone wolf jihadists can use to conduct their attacks, Gadahn notes that while Hasan used firearms in his assault at Fort Hood, jihadists are "no longer limited to bullets and bombs" when it comes to weapons. "As the blessed operations of September 11th showed, a little imagination and planning and a minimal budget can turn almost anything into a deadly, effective and convenient weapon which can take the enemy by surprise and deprive him of sleep for years on end."

Gadahn then turns his attention to targeting. He counsels lone wolf jihadists to follow a three-pronged target selection process. They should choose a target with which they are well acquainted, a target that is feasible to hit and a target that, when struck, will have a major impact. He notes that Hasan's choice of Fort Hood fit all three criteria, but that jihadists should not think that military bases are the only high-value targets in the United States or other Western countries. "On the contrary," Gadahn insists, "there are countless other strategic places, institutions and installations which, by striking, the Muslim can do major damage."

He then says that jihadists must attempt to "further undermine the West's already-struggling economies" by carefully timed and targeted attacks against symbols of capitalism in an effort to "shake consumer confidence and stifle spending." (In this way, Gadahn's message tracks with past messages of Osama bin Laden pertaining to economic jihad.) Gadahn notes that even apparently unsuccessful attacks on Western mass-transportation systems can bring major cities to a halt, cost billions of dollars and send corporations into bankruptcy. He also calls upon jihadists to kill or capture "leading Crusaders and Zionists in government, industry and media."

To summarize his lessons on targeting, Gadahn urges jihadists to "look for targets which epitomize Western decadence, depravity, immorality and atheism — targets which the enemy and his mouthpieces will have trouble trying to pass off to the conservative Muslim majority as illegitimate targets full of innocent people."

Implications

First, it is significant that Gadahn, a representative of the core al Qaeda group, is openly advocating a tactical approach to terrorist attacks that was first publicly laid out by the leader of one of the al Qaeda franchise groups. Nasir al-Wahayshi, head of al Qaeda in the Arabian Peninsula (AQAP), authored an article that appeared in AQAP's Sada al-Malahim online magazine in October 2009 that encouraged jihadists to conduct simple attacks with readily available weapons. Since that time, al-Wahayshi's group has been linked to Hasan and the Fort Hood shooting, the attempt to destroy Northwest Airlines Flight 253 on Christmas Day 2009 and the June 1, 2009, attack against an armed forces recruitment center in Little Rock, Ark. Normally it is the al Qaeda core group that sets the agenda in the jihadist realm, but the success of AQAP has apparently caused the core group to jump on the AQAP bandwagon and endorse al-Wahayshi's approach.

It is also telling that the core al Qaeda group chose to produce this particular video message using Gadahn as the spokesman and not one of their other talking heads like Ayman al-Zawahiri or Abu Yahya al-Libi. Gadahn, an American, is often used by the group to address the West, and English speaking-people in particular, so it is clear that the intended audience for his message was aspiring grassroots jihadists in the West. Indeed, Gadahn says in the video that his message is meant particularly for jihadists in the United States, United Kingdom and Israel. Presented in English, Gadahn's video is more easily accessible to English-speakers than al-Wahayshi's article, which was written in Arabic. Even though the al Qaeda core has been marginalized on the physical battlefield, when it comes to areas like militant philosophy, the pronouncements of the core group carry more influence with the wider jihadist world than statements from a regional franchise such as AQAP. When these two factors are combined, it is reasonable to assume that more people in the English-speaking world may pay attention to this call to simple attacks than they did to al-Wahayshi's call in October 2009. Video is also a more viral type of media than the printed word, and video messages are known to be very appealing to aspiring jihadists.

Another thing this video reveals is the continued weakening of the core al Qaeda group. It has come a long way from the early days of As-Sahab, when bin Laden and other al Qaeda leaders issued defiant threats of launching a follow-on attack against the United States that was going to be even more destructive than 9/11. The group is now asking individual Muslims to conduct lone-wolf terrorist attacks and to follow the examples of Hasan and Mir Amal Kansi, the Pakistani citizen who conducted a shooting at a stoplight outside CIA headquarters in January 1993 that killed two CIA employees. STRATFOR has long been tracking the devolution of the jihadist threat from one primarily based upon al Qaeda the group to one based upon a wider jihadist movement, and this video is a clear indication that the trend toward decentralization is continuing.

This decentralization means grassroots operatives will continue to be a concern. The problems posed by such operatives are illustrated by recent cases involving American citizens like Colleen LaRose (aka Jihad Jane), Jamie Paulin-Ramirez and Sharif Mobley, who are all alleged to have been involved in recent jihadist plots. As blonde Caucasian women, LaRose and Paulin-Ramirez, in particular, do not fit the jihadist operative stereotype in most people's minds and serve to illustrate the difficulty of creating a terrorist profile based on race, ethnicity or gender.

But decentralization can also mean diminished capability. Counseling jihadists against traveling to training camps in places like Pakistan or Yemen and advising them not to coordinate their attacks with others will increase a group's operational security, but it can also have a serious impact on its operational effectiveness. Traditionally, one of the biggest problems for lone-wolf operators is acquiring the skills necessary to conduct a successful terrorist attack. Even though many Web sites and military manuals can provide instruction on such things as hand-to-hand combat and marksmanship, there is no substitute for hands-on experience in the real world. This is especially true when it comes to the more subtle skills required to conduct a complex terrorist attack, such as planning, surveillance and bomb making. This difficulty in translating intent into effective action explains why so few lone-wolf militants have been able to pull off spectacular, mass-casualty attacks.

Not putting their recruits through a more formal training regimen also makes it more difficult for groups to thoroughly indoctrinate recruits with jihadist ideology. In addition to physical training, individuals attending jihadist training camps typically receive hours of theological instruction every day that is intended to ground them in jihadist doctrine and motivate them to follow through with their plans to engage in attacks.

All that said, while the threat posed by grassroots jihadists is less severe than that posed by trained militant operatives from the core al Qaeda group or the regional franchises, grassroots operatives can still kill people — and they most certainly will continue to do so. Because of this, it is important to pay careful attention to the targeting criteria that Gadahn lays out. His focus on mass transportation targets means that historical jihadist targets such as airliners and subways continue to be at risk. For corporate security directors and the protective security details assigned to safeguard high-profile government officials and private individuals, the video should also serve as a reminder of the need to be vigilant. This is doubly true for those assigned to protect individuals of the Jewish faith, who could be thought to fit both the "Crusader" and "Zionist" labels in the mind of a prospective attacker.

For security personnel, the silver lining in all this is that grassroots operatives are often lacking in street skills and tend to be very sloppy when conducting preoperational surveillance. This means that, while these individuals are in many ways more difficult to identify before an attack than operatives who communicate with, or are somehow connected to, jihadist groups (indeed, lone wolves can seemingly appear out of nowhere), their amateurish methods tend to make them more vulnerable to detection than their better-trained counterparts. This is the paradox presented by this class of militant operative — and it is a paradox that will confront security, intelligence and law enforcement officers for many years to come.

Jihadism and the Importance of Place
March 25, 2010

One of the basic tenets of STRATFOR's analytical model is that place matters. A country's physical and cultural geography will force the government of that country to confront certain strategic imperatives no matter what form the government takes. For example, Imperial Russia, the Soviet Union and post-Soviet Russia all faced the same set of strategic imperatives. Similarly, place can also have a dramatic impact on the formation and operation of a militant group, though obviously not in quite the same way that it affects a government, since militant groups, especially transnational ones, tend to be itinerant and can move from place to place.

From the perspective of a militant group, geography is important but there are other critical factors involved in establishing the suitability of a place. While it is useful to have access to wide swaths of rugged terrain that can provide sanctuary such as mountains, jungles or swamps, for a militant group to conduct large-scale operations, the country in which it is based must have a weak central government — or a government that is cooperative or at least willing to turn a blind eye to the group. A sympathetic population is also a critical factor in whether an area can serve as a sanctuary for a militant group. In places without a favorable mixture of these elements, militants tend to operate more like terrorists, in small urban-based cells.

For example, although Egypt was one of the ideological cradles of jihadism, jihadist militants have never been able to gain a solid foothold in Egypt (as they have been able to do in Algeria, Yemen and Pakistan). This is because the combination of geography and government is not favorable to them even in areas of the country where there is a sympathetic population. When jihadist organizations have become active in Egypt, the Egyptian government has been able to quickly hunt them down. Having no place to hide, those militants who are not immediately arrested or killed frequently leave the country and end up in places like Sudan, Iraq, Pakistan (and sometimes

Jersey City). Over the past three decades, many of these itinerant Egyptian militants, such as Ayman al-Zawahiri, have gone on to play significant roles in the formation and evolution of al Qaeda — a stateless, transnational jihadist organization.

Even though al Qaeda and the broader jihadist movement it has sought to foster are transnational, they are still affected by the unique dynamics of place, and it is worth examining how these dynamics will likely affect the movement's future.

The Past

The modern iteration of the jihadist phenomenon that resulted in the formation of al Qaeda was spawned in the rugged mountainous area along the Afghan-Pakistani border. This was a remote region not only filled with refugees — and militants from all over the globe — but also awash in weapons, spies, fundamentalist Islamism and intrigue. The area proved ideal for the formation of modern jihadism following the Soviet withdrawal from Afghanistan in 1989, but it was soon plunged into Muslim-on-Muslim violence. After the fall of the communist regime in Kabul in 1992, Afghanistan was wracked by near-constant civil war between competing Muslim warlords until the Taliban seized power in 1996. Even then, the Taliban-led government remained at war with the Northern Alliance. In 1992, in the midst of this chaos, al Qaeda began to move many of its people to Sudan, which had taken a heavy Islamist bent following a 1989 coup led by Gen. Omar al-Bashir and heavily influenced by Hasan al-Turabi and his National Islamic Front party. Even during this time, al Qaeda continued operating established training camps in Afghanistan like Khaldan, al Farook and Darunta. The group also maintained its network of Pakistani safe-houses in places like Karachi and Peshawar that it used to direct prospective jihadists from overseas to its training camps in Afghanistan.

In many ways, Sudan was a better place for al Qaeda to operate from, since it offered far more access to the outside world than the remote camps in Afghanistan. But the access worked both ways, and the group received far more scrutiny during its time in Sudan than it had during its stay in Afghanistan. In fact, it was during the Sudan years (1992-1996) when many in the counterterrorism world first became conscious of the existence of al Qaeda. Most people outside of the counterterrorism community were not familiar with the group until after the August 1998 East Africa embassy bombings, and it was not really until 9/11 that al Qaeda became a household name. But this notoriety came with a price. Following the June 1995 attempt to assassinate Egyptian President Hosni Mubarak in Addis Ababa, Ethiopia (an attack linked to Egyptian militants and al Qaeda), the international community — including Egypt and the United States — began to place heavy pressure on the government of Sudan to either control Osama bin Laden and al Qaeda or eject them from the country.

In May 1996, bin Laden and company, who were not willing to be controlled, pulled up stakes and headed back to Afghanistan. The timing was propitious for al Qaeda, which was able to find sanctuary in Afghanistan just as the Taliban were preparing for their final push on Kabul, bringing stability to much of the country. While the Taliban were never wildly supportive of bin Laden, they at least tolerated his presence and activities and felt obligated to protect him as their guest under Pashtunwali, the ancient code of the Pashtun people. Al Qaeda also shrewdly had many of its members marry into influential local tribes as an added measure of security. Shortly after returning to Afghanistan, bin Laden felt secure enough to issue his August 1996 declaration of war against the United States.

The rugged and remote region of eastern and northeastern Afghanistan, bordered by the Pakistani badlands, provided an ideal area in which to operate. It was also a long way from the ocean and the United States' ability to project power. While al Qaeda's stay in Afghanistan was briefly interrupted by a U.S. cruise missile attack in August 1998 following the East Africa embassy bombings, the largely ineffective attack demonstrated the limited reach of the United States, and the group was able to operate pretty much unmolested in Afghanistan until the October 2001 U.S. invasion of Afghanistan.

During their time in Afghanistan, al Qaeda was able to provide basic military training to tens of thousands of men who passed through its training camps. The camps also provided advanced training in terrorist tradecraft to a smaller number of selected students.

The U.S. invasion of Afghanistan radically changed the way the jihadists viewed Afghanistan as a place. U.S. military power was no longer confined to the Indian Ocean; it had now been brought right into the heart of Afghanistan. Instead of a place of refuge and training, Afghanistan once again became a place of active combat, and the training camps in Afghanistan were destroyed or relocated to the Pakistani side of the border. Other jihadist refugees fled Afghanistan for their countries of origin, and still others, like Abu Musab al-Zarqawi, left Afghanistan for the badlands of northern Iraq — which, as part of the U.S. no-fly zone, was out of the reach of Saddam Hussein, who as a secular leader had little ideological sympathy for the jihadist cause.

Pakistan's rugged and remote Pashtun belt proved a welcoming refuge for jihadists at first, but U.S. airstrikes turned it into a dangerous place, and al Qaeda became fractured and hunted. The group had lost important operational leaders like Mohammed Atef in Afghanistan, and its losses were multiplied in Pakistan, where important figures like Khalid Sheikh Mohammed were captured or killed. Under extreme pressure, the group's apex leadership went deep underground to stay alive.

Following the U.S. invasion of Iraq in March 2003, Iraq became an important place for the jihadist movement. Unlike Afghanistan, which was seen as remote and on the periphery of the Muslim world, Iraq was at its heart. Baghdad had served as the seat of the Islamic empire for some five centuries. The 2003 invasion also fit hand-in-glove with the jihadist narrative, which claimed that the West had declared war on Islam, and thereby provided a serious boost to efforts to raise men and money for the jihadist struggle. Soon foreign jihadists were streaming into Iraq from all over the world, not only from places like Saudi Arabia and Algeria but also from North America and Europe. Indeed, we even saw the core al Qaeda group asking the Iraqi jihadist leader, Abu Musab al-Zarqawi, for financial assistance.

One of the things that made Iraq such a welcoming place was the hospitality of the Sunni sheikhs in Iraq's Sunni Triangle who took in the foreign fighters, sheltered them and essentially used them as a tool. Once the largesse of these tribal leaders dried up, we saw the Anbar Awakening in 2005-2006, and Iraq became a far more hostile place for the foreign jihadists. This local hostility was fanned by the brutality of al-Zarqawi and his recklessness in attacking other Muslims. The nature of the human terrain had changed in the Sunni Triangle, and it became a different place. Al-Zarqawi was killed in June 2006, and the rat lines that had been moving jihadists into Iraq were severely disrupted.

While some of the jihadists who had served in Iraq, or who had aspired to travel to Iraq, were forced to go to Pakistan, still others began focusing on places like Algeria and Yemen. Shortly after the Anbar Awakening we saw the formation of al Qaeda in the Islamic Maghreb (AQIM) and a revitalization of the jihadists in Yemen, who had been severely weakened by a November 2002 U.S. missile strike and a series of arrests in 2002-2003. Similarly, Somalia also became a destination where foreign jihadists could receive training and fight, especially those of Somali or other African heritage.

And this brings us up to today. The rugged borderlands of Pakistan continue to be a focal point for jihadists, but increasing pressure by U.S. airstrikes and Pakistani military operations in places like Bajaur, Swat and South Waziristan have forced many foreign jihadists to leave Pakistan for safer locations. The al Qaeda central leadership continues to lay low, and groups like the Taliban and al Qaeda in the Arabian Peninsula (AQAP) have taken over the leadership of the jihadist struggle on the physical battlefield. As long as the ideology of jihadism persists, transnational and itinerant jihadist militants will continue to operate. Where their next geographic center of gravity will be hinges on a number of factors.

Geographic Factors

When one looks for prime jihadist real estate, one of the first important factors (as in any real estate transaction) is location. Unlike most homebuyers, though, jihadists don't want a home near the metro stop or important commuter arteries. Instead, they want a place that is isolated and relatively free of government authority. That is why Afghanistan, the Pakistani border region, the Sulu Archipelago, the African Sahel and Somalia have all proved to be popular jihadist haunts.

A second important factor is human terrain. Like any militant or insurgent group, the jihadists need a local population that is sympathetic to them if they are to operate in numbers larger than small cells. This is especially true if they hope to run operations such as training camps that are hard to conceal. Without local support, they would run the risk of being turned in to the authorities or sold out to countries like the United States that may have put large bounties on the heads of key leaders. A conservative Muslim population with a warrior tradition is also a plus, as seen in Pakistan and Yemen. Indeed, Abu Musab al-Suri, a well-known jihadist strategist and so-called "architect of global jihad," even tried (unsuccessfully) to convince bin Laden in 1989 to relocate to Yemen precisely because of the favorable human terrain there.

The importance of human terrain is very evident in the Iraq example described above, in which a change in attitude by the tribal sheikhs rapidly made once welcoming areas into hostile and dangerous places for the foreign jihadists. Iraqi jihadists, who were able to fit in better with the local population, were able to persist in this hostile environment longer than their foreign counterparts. This concept of local support is one of the factors that will limit the ability of Arab jihadists to operate in remote and chaotic places like sub-Saharan Africa or even the rainforests of South America. They are not indigenous like members of the Revolutionary Armed Forces of Colombia or Sendero Luminoso, and differences in religion and culture will impede their efforts to intermarry into powerful tribes as they have done in Pakistan and Yemen.

Geography and human terrain are helpful factors, but they are not the exclusive determinants. You can just as easily train militants in an open field as in a dense jungle, so long as you are unmolested by an outside force, and that is why government is so important to place. A weak government that has a lack of political and physical control over an area or a local regime that is either cooperative or at least non-interfering is also important. When we consider government, we need to focus on the ability and will of the government at the local level to fight an influx of jihadism. In several countries, jihadism was allowed to exist and was not countered by the government as long as the jihadists focused their efforts elsewhere.

However, the wisdom of pursuing such an approach came into question in the period following 9/11, when jihadist groups in a number of places began conducting active operations in their countries of residence. This occurred in places like Indonesia, Saudi Arabia, Morocco and even Egypt's Sinai Peninsula, where jihadist groups joined al Qaeda's call for a global jihad. And this response proved to be very costly for these groups. The attacks they conducted, combined with heavy political pressure from the United States, forced some governments to change the way they viewed the groups and resulted in some governments focusing the full weight of their power to destroy them. This resulted in a dynamic where a group briefly appears, makes a splash with some spectacular attacks, then is dismantled by the local government, often with foreign assistance (from countries like the United States). In some countries, the governments lacked the necessary intelligence-gathering and tactical capabilities, and it has taken a lot of time and effort to build up those capabilities for the counterterrorism struggle. In other places, like Somalia, there has been very little government to build on.

Since the 9/11 attacks, the U.S. government has paid a lot of attention to "draining the swamps" where these groups seek refuge and train new recruits. This effort has spanned the globe, from the southern Philippines to Central Asia and from Bangladesh to Mali and Mauritania. And it is paying off in places like Yemen, where some of the special counterterrorism forces are starting to exhibit some self-sufficiency and have begun to make headway against AQAP. If Yemen continues to exhibit the will to go after AQAP, and if the international community continues to enable them to do so, it will be able to follow the examples of Morocco, Saudi Arabia and Indonesia, countries where the jihadist problem has not been totally eradicated but where the groups are hunted and their tactical capabilities are greatly diminished. This will mean that Yemen will no longer be seen as a jihadist haven and training base. The swamp there will have been mostly drained. Another significant part of this effort will be to reshape the human terrain through ideological measures. These include discrediting jihadism as an ideology, changing the curriculum at madrassas and re-educating militants.

With swamps such as Yemen and Pakistan slowly being drained, the obvious question is: Where will the jihadists go next? What will become the next focal point on the physical battlefield? One obvious location is Somalia, but while the government there is a basket case and controls little more than a few neighborhoods in Mogadishu, the environment is not very conducive for Somalia to become the next Pakistan or Yemen. While the human terrain in Somalia is largely made up of conservative Muslims, the tribal divisions and fractured nature of Somali society — the same things that keep the government from being able to develop any sort of cohesion — will also work against al- Shabaab and its jihadist kin. Many of the various tribal chieftains and territorial warlords see the jihadists as a threat to their power and will therefore fight them — or leak intelligence to the United States, enabling it to target jihadists it views as a threat. Arabs and South Asians also tend to stick out in Somalia, which is a predominately black country.

Moreover, Somalia, like Yemen, has broad exposure to the sea, allowing the United States more or less direct access. With Somalia's long shorelines along the Indian Ocean and the Gulf of Aden, it is comparatively easy to slip aircraft and even special operations teams into and out of the country. With a U.S. base in Djibouti, orbits of unmanned aerial vehicles are also easy to sustain in Somali airspace. The winnowing down of places for jihadists to gather and train in large numbers continues the long process we have been following for many years now. This is the transition of the jihadist threat from one based on al Qaeda the group, or even on its regional franchise groups, to one based more on a wider movement composed of smaller grassroots cells and lone-wolf operatives. Going forward, the fight against jihadism will also have to adapt, because the changes in the threat will force a shift in focus from merely trying to drain the big swamps to mopping up the little pools of jihadists in places like London, Brooklyn, Karachi and even cyberspace. As discussed last week, this fight will present its own set of challenges.

From Failed Bombings to Armed Assaults
May 27, 2010

One of the things we like to do from time to time is examine the convergence of a number of separate and unrelated developments and then analyze that convergence and craft a forecast. In recent months, we have seen such a convergence occur.

The most recent development is the interview with the American-born Yemeni cleric Anwar al-Awlaki that was released to jihadist Internet chat rooms May 23 by al-Malahim Media, the public relations arm of al Qaeda in the Arabian Peninsula (AQAP). In the interview, al-Awlaki encouraged strikes against American civilians. He also has been tied to U.S. Army Maj. Nidal Hasan, who was charged in the November 2009 Fort Hood shooting, and Umar Farouk Abdulmutallab, the perpetrator of the failed Christmas Day 2009 airline bombing. And al-Awlaki reportedly helped inspire Faisal Shahzad, who was arrested in connection with the attempted Times Square attack in May.

The second link in our chain is the failed Christmas Day and Times Square bombings themselves. They are the latest in a long string of failed or foiled bombing attacks directed against the United States that date back to before the 9/11 attacks and include the thwarted 1997 suicide bomb plot against a subway in New York, the thwarted December 1999 Millennium Bomb plot and numerous post-9/11 attacks such as Richard Reid's December 2001 shoe-bomb attempt, the August 2004 plot to bomb the New York subway system and the May 2009 plot to bomb two Jewish targets in the Bronx and shoot down a military aircraft. Indeed, jihadists have not conducted a successful bombing attack inside the United States since the 1993 World Trade Center bombing. Getting a trained bomb maker into the United States has proved to be increasingly difficult for jihadist groups, and training a novice to make bombs has also been problematic as seen in the Shahzad and Najibullah Zazi cases.

The final link we'd like to consider are the calls in the past few months for jihadists to conduct simple attacks with readily available items. This call was first made by AQAP leader Nasir al-Wahayshi in October 2009 and then echoed by al Qaeda-prime spokesman Adam Gadahn in March 2010. In the Times Square case, Shahzad did use readily available items, but he lacked the ability to effectively fashion them into a viable explosive device.

When we look at all these links together, there is a very high probability that jihadists linked to, or inspired by, AQAP and the Tehrik-i-Taliban Pakistan (TTP) — and perhaps even al Shabaab — will attempt to conduct simple attacks with firearms in the near future.

Threats and Motives

In the May 23 al-Malahim interview (his first with AQAP), al-Awlaki not only said he was proud of the actions of Hasan and Abdulmutallab, whom he referred to as his students, but also encouraged other Muslims to follow the examples they set by their actions. When asked about the religious permissibility of an operation like Abdulmutallab's, which could have killed innocent civilians, al-Awlaki told the interviewer that the term "civilian" was not really applicable to Islamic jurisprudence and that he preferred to use the terms combatants and non-combatants. He then continued by noting that "non-combatants are people who do not take part in the war" but that, in his opinion, "the American people in its entirety takes part in the war, because they elected this administration, and they finance this war." In his final assessment, al-Awlaki said, "If the heroic mujahid brother Umar Farouk could have targeted hundreds of soldiers, that would have been wonderful. But we are talking about the realities of war," meaning that in his final analysis, attacks against civilians were permissible under Islamic law. Indeed, he later noted, "Our unsettled account with America, in women and children alone, has exceeded one million. Those who would have been killed in the plane are a drop in the ocean."

While this line of logic is nearly identical to that historically put forth by Osama bin Laden and Ayman al-Zawahiri, the very significant difference is that al-Awlaki is a widely acknowledged Islamic scholar. He speaks with a religious authority that bin Laden and al-Zawahiri simply do not possess.

On May 2, the TTP released a video statement by Hakeemullah Mehsud in which Mehsud claimed credit for the failed Times Square attack. In the recording, which reportedly was taped in early April, Mehsud said that the time was approaching "when our fedayeen [suicide operatives] will attack the American states in their major cities." He also said, "Our fedayeen have penetrated the terrorist America. We will give extremely painful blows to the fanatic America."

While TTP leaders seem wont to brag and exaggerate (e.g., Baitullah Mehsud falsely claimed credit for the April 3, 2009, shooting at an immigration center in Binghamton, N.Y., which was actually committed by a mentally disturbed Vietnamese immigrant), there is ample reason to believe the claims made by the TTP regarding their contact with Shahzad. We can also deduce with some certainty that Mehsud and company have trained other men who have traveled (or returned) to the United States following that training. The same is likely true for AQAP, al Shabaab and other jihadist groups. In fact, the FBI is likely monitoring many such individuals inside the United States at this very moment — and in all likelihood is scrambling to find and investigate many others.

Fight Like You Train

There is an old military and law-enforcement training axiom that states, "You will fight like you train." This concept has led to the development of training programs designed to help soldiers and agents not only learn skills but also practice and reinforce those skills until they become second nature. This way, when the student graduates and comes under incredible pressure in the real world — like during an armed ambush — their training will take over and they will react even before their mind can catch up to the rapidly unfolding situation. The behaviors needed to survive have been ingrained into them. This concept has been a problem for the jihadists when it comes to terrorist attacks.

It is important to understand that most of the thousands of men who attend training camps set up by al Qaeda and other jihadist groups are taught the basic military skills required to fight in an insurgency. This means they are provided basic physical training to help condition them, given some hand-to-hand combat training and then taught how to operate basic military hardware like assault rifles, hand grenades and, in some cases, crew-served weapons like machine guns and mortars. Only a very few students are then selected to attend the more advanced training that will teach them the skills required to become a trained terrorist operative.

In many ways, this process parallels the way that special operations forces operators are selected from the larger military population and then sent on for extensive training to transform them into elite warriors. Many people wash out during this type of intense training and only a few will make it all the way through to graduation. The problem for the jihadists is finding someone with the time and will to undergo the intensive training required to become a terrorist operative, the ability to complete the training and — critically — the ability to travel abroad to conduct terrorist attacks against the far enemy. Clearly the jihadist groups are able to train men to fight as insurgents in Afghanistan and Iraq, and they have shown the ability to train terrorist operatives who can operate in the fairly permissive environments of places like the Afghan-Pakistani border area. They also have some excellent bomb makers and terrorist planners in Iraq and Pakistan.

What the jihadists seem to be having a problem doing is finding people who can master the terrorist tradecraft and who have the ability to travel into hostile areas to ply their trade. There seems to be a clear division between the men who can travel and the men who can master the advanced training. The physical and intelligence onslaught launched against al Qaeda and other jihadist groups following the 9/11 attacks has also created operational security concerns that complicate the ability to find and train effective terrorist operatives.

Of course, we're not telling the jihadists anything they don't already know. This phenomenon is exactly why you have major jihadist figures like al-Wahayshi and Gadahn telling the operatives who can travel to or are already in the West to stop trying to conduct attacks that are beyond their capabilities. Gadahn and al-Awlaki have heaped praise on Maj. Hasan as an example to follow — and this brings us back to armed assaults.

In the United States, it is very easy to obtain firearms, and it is legal to go to a range or private property to train with them. Armed assaults are also clearly within the skill set of jihadists who have made it only through basic insurgent training. As we've mentioned several times in the past, these grassroots individuals are far more likely to strike the United States and Europe than professional terrorist operatives dispatched from the al Qaeda core group. Such attacks will also allow these grassroots operatives to fight like they have been trained. When you combine all these elements with the fact that the United States is an open society with a lot of very vulnerable soft targets, it is not difficult to forecast that we will see more armed jihadist assaults in the United States in the near future.

Armed Assaults

Armed assaults employing small arms are not a new concept in terrorism by any means. They have proved to be a tried-and-true tactic since the beginning of the modern era of terrorism and have been employed in many famous attacks conducted by a variety of actors. A few examples are the Black September operation against the Israeli athletes at the 1972 Munich Olympics; the December 1975 seizure of the Organization of the Petroleum Exporting Countries headquarters in Vienna, led by Ilich Ramirez Sanchez, aka "Carlos the Jackal"; the December 1985 simultaneous attacks against the airports in Rome and Vienna by the Abu Nidal Organization; and the September 2004 school seizure in Beslan, North Ossetia, by Chechen militants. More recently, the November 2008 armed assault in Mumbai demonstrated how deadly and spectacular such attacks can be.

In some instances, such as the December 1996 seizure of the Japanese ambassador's residence in Lima, Peru, by the Tupac Amaru Revolutionary Movement, the objective of the armed assault is to take and intentionally hold hostages for a long period of time. In other instances, such as the May 1972 assault on Lod Airport by members of the Japanese Red Army, the armed assault is planned as a suicide attack designed simply to kill as many people as possible before the assailants themselves are killed or incapacitated. Often attacks fall somewhere in the middle. For example, even though Mumbai became a protracted operation, its planning and execution indicated it was intended as an attack in which the attackers would inflict maximum damage and not be taken alive. It was only due to the good fortune of the attackers and the ineptitude of the Indian security forces that the operation lasted as long as it did.

We discussed above the long string of failed and foiled bombing attacks directed against the United States. During that same time, there have been several armed assaults that have killed people, such as the attack against the El Al ticket counter at the Los Angeles International Airport by Hesham Mohamed Hadayet in July 2002, the shooting attacks by John Muhammad and Lee Boyd Malvo in the

Washington area in September and October 2002 and the June 2009 attack in which Abdulhakim Mujahid Muhammad allegedly shot and killed a U.S. soldier and wounded another outside a Little Rock, Ark., recruiting center. The most successful of these attacks was the November 2009 Fort Hood shooting, which resulted in 13 deaths. These attacks not only resulted in deaths but also received extensive media coverage.

Armed assaults are effective and they can kill people. However, as we have noted before, due to the proficiency of U.S. police agencies and the training their officers have received in active-shooter scenarios following school shootings and incidents of workplace violence, the impact of armed assaults will be mitigated in the United States, and Europe as well. In fact, it was an ordinary police officer responding to the scene and instituting an active-shooter protocol who shot and wounded Maj. Hasan and brought an end to his attack in the Soldier Readiness Center at Fort Hood. The number of people in the American public who are armed can also serve as a mitigating factor, though many past attacks have been planned at locations where personal weapons are prohibited, like the Los Angeles International Airport, Fort Hood and Fort Dix.

Of course, a Mumbai-like situation involving multiple trained shooters who can operate like a fire team will cause problems for first responders, but the police communication system in the United States and the availability of trained SWAT teams will allow authorities to quickly vector in sufficient resources to handle the threat in most locations — especially where such large coordinated attacks are most likely to happen, such as New York, Washington and Los Angeles. Therefore, even a major assault in the United States is unlikely to drag out for days as did the incident in Mumbai.

None of this is to say that the threats posed by suicide bombers against mass transit and aircraft will abruptly end. The jihadists have proved repeatedly that they have a fixation on both of these target sets and they will undoubtedly continue their attempts to attack them. Large bombings and airline attacks also carry with them a sense of drama that a shooting does not — especially in a country that has become somewhat accustomed to shooting incidents conducted by non-terrorist actors for other reasons. However, we believe we're seeing a significant shift in the mindset of jihadist ideologues and that this shift will translate into a growing trend toward armed assaults.

www.ingramcontent.com/pod-product-compliance
Lightning Source LLC
Chambersburg PA
CBHW062144280526
45788CB00001B/298